the Wh...

POET

SHROPSHIRE

Edited by Allison Dowse

First published in Great Britain in 2003 by
YOUNG WRITERS
Remus House,
Coltsfoot Drive,
Peterborough, PE2 9JX
Telephone (01733) 890066

HB ISBN 0 75434 249 2
SB ISBN 0 75434 250 6

FOREWORD

This year, the Young Writers' The Write Stuff! competition proudly presents a showcase of the best poetic talent from over 40,000 up-and-coming writers nationwide.

Young Writers was established in 1991 and we are still successful, even in today's modern world, in promoting and encouraging the reading and writing of poetry.

The thought, effort, imagination and hard work put into each poem impressed us all, and once again, the task of selecting poems was a difficult one, but nevertheless, an enjoyable experience.

We hope you are as pleased as we are with the final selection and that you and your family continue to be entertained with *The Write Stuff! Shropshire* for many years to come.

Contents

Rachael Grimshaw	21
Lewis Jones	21
Christy Matta	22
Matthew Onions	22
Merryn Kelly	23
Bethany Alcock	23
Melissa Bailey	24
Laura Markland	24
Joseph Clutton	25
Sian Jones	25
Shelly Ashman	26
James Hill	26
Stephanie Leach	26
Amy Fletcher	27
Emma Fletcher	28

Charlton School

Amelia McCabe	29

Madeley Court School

Melissa Grindrod	30
Kirk Smith	31
Daniel Sherry	31
Athena Lill	32
Georgina Kilford	32
Nicola Little	33
Elizabeth Smith	33
Sarah Morris	34
Lauren Jones	34
Sammy Blake	34
Janine Unwin & Stacey Bevan	35
Jason Smith	35
Nathan Hammond	35
Kelsey McClean & Stacey Winton	36

Meole Brace School

Katie Davies	36
Peter Landers	37

Sean Martin	59
Natasha Hall	60
Billy Church	61
Charlie Ashton	62
Claire Owen	62
Alex Cameron	63
Robert Griffiths	63
Ed Mainwaring	64
Ruby Honnor	64
Sean Willis	65
Claudette C Williamson	65
Lucy Alexander	66
Tom Williams	66
Tom Law	67
Fern Owen	68
Emma Hartley	68
Rosanna Urwick	69
Louise Turner	69
Jospeh Ruxton	70
Ani Gallagher-Walker	70
Claire Macklin	71
Sam Stone	72
Jessica Sanders	72
Andrew Kirby	73
David Seadon	73
James Brett	74
Mazin Abdelaziz	74
David Phillips	75
David Hall	76
Elizabeth Davies	76
Stacey Jones	77
Cameron Rose	78
Nick Humphreys	79
Andrew Stott	80
Fiona Edwards	80
Matthew Coey	81
Lauren Shannon	82
David Griffiths	82

Mark Young	83
Emily Smith	83
Amy Williams	84
Danny Williams	84
Rick Keville	85
Danny Sadd	86
Emma Thomas	86
Amy Fry	87
Matthew Pope	88
Alice Johnson	88
Romany Nutland	89
Alison Hosker	90
Sam Sherwin	90
Emma Bailey	91
Lizzie Stephens	92
Rowan Connolly	93
Abigail Edwards	94
Rachel Tree	94
Ben Hughes	95
Alex Newcombe-Rose	96
Phoebe Pickard	97
Chris James	97
Sarah Guthrie	98
Ben Humphreys	98
Naomi Stokes	99
James Hickson	99
Valentina Biuso	100
Kate Almond	100
Becky Hanlon	101
Katie Green	102
Joe Hosty	102
Lewis Pollock	103
Sarah Beedles	104
Alice O'Donoghue	104
Naomi Scott	105

The Mary Webb School

Samantha Williams	105
Keri Daniel	106
Leanne Hughes	106
Claire Vernon	107
Alex Capewell	108
Emily Roberts	108
Luanne Bellis	109
Lucy Price	110
Sally Poole	110
Emma Marshall	111
Matthew Donnelly	112
Oliver Parry	112
Ky Holder	113
Jemma Pearson	114
Verity Scholes	115
Simon Glover	115
Connor Grady	116
Vicki Richardson	116
Andrew Keegan	117
Christopher Ballard	118

The Phoenix School

Nikita Soltys	118
Shaun Evans	119
Jonathan Hull	119
Holly Deans	120
Vicki Cork	120
Leanne Gray	121
James Rowley	121
Scott Biddulph	122
Jack Welch	122
Lucy Fletcher	123
Tom Higginson	123
Jack Eveson	124
Simon Phillips	124
Louise Pickering	125
Emma Childs	125

The Poems

HALLOWE'EN

At 12 the clock struck
it was night
the moon was whole,
cloudy sky,
it was Hallowe'en.
The spiders took
nearly all night,
the witches came
to play a game,
the wolves howled,
ghosts walked through the walls
they had no shadows at all.
Pumpkins bright
with a light
as the midnight party begun
just before the sun.
After six everything gone,
silent now
until next Hallowe'en.

Alicya Oakes (12)
Abraham Darby School

THE MAN FROM CHINA

There was a man from China
He wasn't a very good climber
He slipped on a rock
Ripped open his sock
That clumsy man from China.

Carl Johnson (11)
Abraham Darby School

SUMMER DAYS

Summer days
We all will praise
Here we sit
Play and gaze.

Red faces
Lie in bed
Wake up time
Sleepyhead.

Birds singing
In the trees,
Feel the air
Of this lovely breeze.

People bathing
In the sun,
Children playing
Having fun.

Summer days
We all will praise,
Here we sit
Play and gaze.

Kallie Sheridon (12)
Abraham Darby School

LIMERICKS

There was a young man from Dundee
Who went to his granny's for tea,
He went really fast
But time never passed
That silly young man from Dundee.

There was a young lady from Bury
Who always walked round in a hurry,
She walked round so fast
She never was last
That silly young lady from Bury.

Sian Evans (11)
Abraham Darby School

I'D LIKE TO BE . . .

I'd like to be an MC
So I could do a funky rap.

I'd like to be a dancer
So I could do funky tap.

I'd like to be a blader
So I could go to the extreme.

I'd like to be a boat boy
So I could sail down the stream.

I'd like to be a judge
So I could throw people in jail.

I'd like to be a lawyer
So I could get people bail.

I'd like to be a doctor
So I could make people better.

I'd like to be a postman
So I could deliver a letter.

Luke Birch (11)
Abraham Darby School

I'D LIKE TO BE . . .

I'd like to be a doctor,
So I could try to mend your back.
I'd like to be an athlete,
So I could run fast on the track.

I'd like to be a postman,
So I could deliver mail.
I'd like to be a hunter,
So I could follow a trail.

I'd like to be a dentist,
So I could hear them scream and shout.
I'd like to be a teacher,
So I could help the children count.

I'd like to be a pilot,
So I could fly to the stars.
I'd like to be an artist,
So I could paint the planet Mars.

Nina Kaur Hamilton (11)
Abraham Darby School

I'D LIKE TO BE . . .

I'd like to be an artist,
So I could paint a perfect cat.
I'd like to be a postman,
So I could wear a big blue hat.

I'd like to be a dentist,
So I could use a great big drill.
I'd like to be a carer,
So I could give someone their pill.

I'd like to be a hunter,
So I could shoot down all those bears.
I'd like to be a welder,
So I could weld people's chairs.

I'd like to be an artist,
So I could sketch, draw and paint.
I'd like to be a doctor,
So I could help you if you faint.

Gemma Welch (11)
Abraham Darby School

I'D LIKE TO BE . . .

I'd like to be an athlete,
So I could run fast on the track.
I'd like to be a doctor,
So I could mend your back.

I'd like to be an artist,
So I could paint wild flowers.
I'd like to be a pop star,
So I could not work long hours.

I'd like to be a robber,
So I could steal the crown jewels.
I'd like to be a welder,
So I could work with lots of tools.

I'd like to be a DJ,
So I could play funky tunes.
I'd like to be a chef,
So I could stir with big wooden spoons.

Jade Emery (11)
Abraham Darby School

I'D LIKE TO BE . . .

I'd like to be a dancer,
So I could dance away the night.
I'd like to be an artist,
So I could look at the moonlight.

I'd like to be a cleaner,
So I could make the mess less.
I'd like to be a baby,
So I could create the biggest mess.

I'd like to be a postman,
So I could walk all day.
I'd like to be a DJ,
So I could play in May all day.

I'd like to be a doctor,
So I could make people better.
I'd like to be a postman,
So I could post all the letters.

Jasvir Kaur (11)
Abraham Darby School

IF I . . .

If I die before you do
I will be there to see you through
If you're not there by Judgement Day
I'll know you went the other way.
So I'll give the angels back their things
Their golden harp, their golden wings
To show my love is true to you
I'll go to Hell to be with you.

Maisie Pugh (11)
Abraham Darby School

I'D LIKE TO BE ...

I'd like to be a hunter,
So I could kill a polar bear.
I'd like to be a barber,
So I could cut off loads of hair.

I'd like to be an athlete,
So I could run fast on the track.
I'd like to be a doctor,
So I could mend your broken back.

I'd like to be a sailor,
So I could sail the seven seas.
I'd like to be a farmer,
So I could look after the bees.

I'd like to be a rugby player,
So I could score lots of goals.
I'd like to be a footballer,
So I could play against Paul Scholes.

Nathan Payton (12)
Abraham Darby School

THE DESERTED HOUSE

Lost and alone, away from home,
Upon the lonely moor,
There is a house, rundown and old,
Hidden by the trees.
Nobody lives there,
No smoke billowing from the chimney,
No laughing children running around,
No little footsteps padding up and down the stairs,
All gone, no more, hidden away, on its own.

Sarah Mason (13)
Abraham Darby School

I'D LIKE TO BE . . .

I'd like to be a soldier,
So I could kill the enemy.

I'd like to be a tourist,
So I could sail over the sea.

I'd like to be a spider,
So I could crawl up the wall.

I'd like to be a goalie,
So I could dive for the football.

I'd like to be a sewer
So I could get lots of dosh.

I'd like to be like Schumacher,
So I could be very posh.

I'd like to be a digger,
So I could dig up lots of bones.

I'd like to be a lawyer,
So I could get loads of loans.

Jimi Duffell (11)
Abraham Darby School

LIMERICKS

There was a young lady from Spain
Who flew very high in a plane
She went up too high
And started to cry
That silly lady from Spain.

There was a young man from Southend
Who drove his friends around the bend
He did not know to stop
So he got some pop
That silly man from Southend.

Michelle Welch (11)
Abraham Darby School

THE PHANTOM!

If you want me to whisper your name
And fill your life with pain.
If you want to travel by train,
Don't forget the emergency chain.

Then wish for me with all your might,
And whisper this three times a night,
> The phantom!
> The phantom!
> The phantom!

If you try to stay up all night,
You'll be given such a fright.
If you find somewhere new to stay,
Just remember you better pray.

Then wish for me with all your might
And whisper this three times a night,
> The phantom!
> The phantom!
> The phantom!

Jodi Stansfield (11)
Abraham Darby School

CELEBRATION OF LIFE

The love, affection,
The kindness not to mention.
Hopes for the future,
Not too near as too far.
It's all happened incredibly quick,
But not too quick for me or my Nick.
The preparing and invites,
So joyful, want to do it all in one night!
Silk, white dresses, make-up and hair,
Already in no time feels like I'm there!
Want wedding bells to ring,
Want the guests to sing.
I want my day to be perfect,
Nothing that disturbs it.
No riots, no fights,
Just drinking of pints.
The vows to be true,
Not just for me but for you.
No secrets be hidden,
Mistakes all forgiven,
But not all, for if you should stumble,
I will be humble!
Marriage should be great,
Opening of a new gate,
To life beyond the present with thy spouse,
And build a stable, honest relationship,
In your chosen home, your house!

Danielle Perkins (14)
Abraham Darby School

I'D LIKE TO BE . . .

I'd like to be a postman,
So I could deliver all the mail.
I'd like to be a policeman,
So I could put my friends in jail.

I'd like to be a DJ,
So I could play snazzy beat.
I'd like to be a doctor,
So I could mess with people's feet.

I'd like to be a singer,
So I could shout down people's ears.
I'd like to be a hunter,
So I could shoot down lots of deers.

I'd like to be a writer,
So I could write a famous book.
I'd like to be an actor,
So I could play Captain Hook.

I'd like to be a dancer,
So I could dance the night away.
I'd like to be a milkman,
So I could deliver milk every day.

I'd like to be a doctor,
So I could make people scream.
I'd like to be an athlete,
So I could live my wildest dream.

Laura Coleman (12)
Abraham Darby School

PHANTOM

If you want me to rattle my chains
And whisper out your surnames

Then whisper this with all your might,
Three times at night,

Ooh the phantom . . .
Ooh phantom . . .
Ooh the phantom . . .

If you want me to give you a fright
And sing a song all the night,

Then whisper this with all your might,
Three times at night,

Ooh the phantom . . .
Ooh phantom . . .
Ooh the phantom . . .

If you want me to fill you with gloom
And float around your bedroom,

Then whisper this with all your might,
Three times at night,

Phantom, I'm not scared of you . . .
No I'm not . . .
Phantom, I'm not scared of you . . .
No I'm not . . .
Phantom, I'm not scared of you . . .
No I'm not!

Are you sure you're not scared?
I can do stuff that you didn't know I could do.
Ha, ha, ha, ha, ha!
Help!

Jodie Hurford (11)
Abraham Darby School

A POEM OF THE NIGHT

When the day is asleep,
A black velvet washes over our world.
Sewn on it is silver sequins
And a bright white button.
When the day is asleep
There is mostly silence
Apart from the hooting of an owl
And if you listen close enough
You might hear the feared wolf,
Howling to its brothers.
When the day is asleep
Creatures of the night out to play.
The bats twirl and dance
And foxes jump and pounce.
All underneath a sky of jewels.
When the day is asleep,
We are tucked up in bed,
With only dreams in our head
And outside another world is living,
Of diamonds and jewels
And we miss it all.

Laura Mahony (14)
Abraham Darby School

I'D LIKE TO BE . . .

I'd like to be a singer,
So I could make a groovy tune.
I'd like to be a lightweight man,
So I could float to the moon.

I'd like to be a dentist,
So I could pull out people's teeth.
I'd like to be an artist,
So I could sketch a pretty leaf.

I'd like to be a monkey,
So I could be so funky.
I'd like to be a Kit-Kat,
So I could be so chunky.

I'd like to be a soldier,
So I could kill so many souls.
I'd like to be a fireman,
So I could slide down loads of poles.

Aaron Simpson (11)
Abraham Darby School

THE SEA

I thought a life at sea
Would be for me
Doing as the sailors do
So one day,
I ran away,
The nearest ship to seek.
But life at sea
Is not for me,
It only made me sick!

Craig Green (11)
Abraham Darby School

I'D LIKE TO BE . . .

I'd like to be a writer
So I could write a famous book.
I'd like to be a fairy
So I could bring people good luck.

I'd like to be a singer
So I could sing a lovely tune.
I'd like to be a pilot
So I could fly across the moon.

I'd like to be a dolphin
So I could swim in the deep blue sea.
I'd like to be a garden
So I could grow a great tree.

Vanda Whittington (11)
Abraham Darby School

BEING YOUNG

When I was young,
I thought I'd live forever,
I believed in ghosts
And thought everyone was clever,
But now I've wised up
And know that none of that's true,
I believe what I say
And understand what I do,
Of course I don't want to die,
I want to banish all pain,
Because when I sleep at night
I dream of being young again.

Camilla Kendrick (13)
Abraham Darby School

I'D LIKE TO BE A . . .

I'd like to be a dancer,
So I can dance through day and night.
I'd like to be a wrestler,
So I can have a vicious fight.

I'd like to be an artist,
So I could paint the lovely moon.
I'd like to be an athlete,
So I can win some races soon.

I'd like to be a postman,
So I can deliver lots of mail.
I'd like to be a teacher,
So I can make my pupils fail.

I'd like to be a cook,
So I can cook some lovely tarts.
I'd like to be a driver,
So I can drive some cool go-karts.

Laura Greenfield (11)
Abraham Darby School

POETRY

P   oetry is a wonderful thing
O   h how I like it so much indeed
E   xciting and fun to sing
T   empting to look at and happily read
R   eading the poem is so enjoyable
Y   oung and old, we love it so much,
    so don't forget to read, read, read.

Sherelle Brown (11)
Abraham Darby School

STORMY WEATHER

Against the sea wall,
The pounding of a drum,
Memories lost in a blanket of oblivion,
Calmness shall come when the wind will not blow,
Once tranquillity, now turmoil,
Once joy, now sorrow,
Once beauty, now grotesque,
Crash, crash, crash,
To the beat of a drum,
Once was great, now in ruins,
Once was fear, now is anger,
Crash, crash, crash,
To the beat of its drum.

Tyler Langan (14)
Abraham Darby School

FUTURE

In the future where will I be?
Will I be with the stars?
Will I live in Aqua Land
Or will I live with you?

Will I be a hero
Or Darth Vader too?
Will I have a Ferrari
Or will I have a bike?

Will I live in might
Or will I live and fight?

Daniel Childe-Freeman (12)
Abraham Darby School

CELEBRATION OF LIFE

I thank God for my family
And happy times they've spent with me.

The love, the life, the happiness,
Yes I know, this is a bless.

The friends that gossip in my ear,
I'm glad my life is right down here.

The twinkle, sparkle in their eye,
When I see it, it makes me cry.

I wouldn't change my world around,
If it changed, my face would frown.

I love them through most anything,
I love the connection that they bring.

At my grave, I want to see
Everybody happily.

But I have to say, thanks to all,
For making my life, great and tall.

Becky Evans (14)
Abraham Darby School

LIMERICK

There was a young man from France
Who got slapped with a pair of pink pants
He shouted out, 'Aaww!'
And woke up a cow
That silly young man from France.

Lauren Rowland (11)
Abraham Darby School

I'D LIKE TO BE . . .

I'd like to be a baker
So I could make lovely cakes.
I'd like to be a doctor
So I could cure people's aches.

I'd like to be an artist
So I could write and draw.
I'd like to be a dancer
So I could break the wooden floor.

I'd like to be a DJ
So I could play funky tunes.
I'd like to be an artist
So I could paint the moon.

I'd like to be a bunny
So I could jump and hop.
I'd like to be a shopper
So I could shop, shop, shop

Sharna Podmore (11)
Abraham Darby School

THE YOUNG MAN FROM JAPAN

There was a young man from Japan,
Who was hit round the head with a pan,
He thought it was great,
To be hit by his mate,
That silly young man from Japan!

Abbie O'Hanlon (12)
Abraham Darby School

LIMERICKS

There was a young lady from Spain
Who got run over by a fast train
She went to Devon
And now she's in Heaven.

There was a young man from Japan
Who brought an expensive fan
He had turned it on
It blew up like a bomb
That silly young man from Japan.

Lee Evans (12)
Abraham Darby School

SCHOOL

S   chool is a place for an education
C   ollege is kind of the same
H   omework is boring
O   ccasional facts too
O   ut of the blue it comes to us
L   earning how to read and write is what we always do.

David Jones (11)
Abraham Darby School

LIMERICKS

There was a young lady from Rome
Who went to the Millennium Dome
She said it was fine
And drank all of her wine
That silly drunk lady went home, from Rome.

Mark Roberts (12)
Abraham Darby School

LIMERICKS

There was a young man from Crockett
Who went up to space in a rocket
The rocket went bang
His belly went twang
And his guts ended up in his pocket.

There was a young lady from Ta Boo
Who needed to go to the loo
She slipped on a tile
And flew for a mile
The silly young lady from Ta Boo.

Mark Whyle (11)
Abraham Darby School

POEMS

P   oems are great
O   h how I love them
E   njoying the rhythms and the short little stories
M   yths and legends and stories too
S   inging and laughing is what makes it true.

Rachael Grimshaw (11)
Abraham Darby School

THAT SILLY YOUNG MAN FROM DUNDEE

There was a young man from Dundee
Who fell madly in love with a bee.
He gave her some honey,
She stole all his money,
That silly young man from Dundee.

Lewis Jones (11)
Abraham Darby School

THE START OF THE DAY

The alarm clock is ringing, it's driving me mad,
'Get up, let's move it!' shouts my dad.
'Wash your face, brush your teeth, let's get on our way.'
Uhh, my dad's always angry at the start of the day.

I grabbed my bag on the way through the door,
Tripped over the cat and fell on the floor.
I think I'm becoming just like my dad,
The start of the day is making me mad.

I climb in the car, finally ready to go
And my dad starts complaining about me being so slow.
I think to myself it's always this way
So much hassle at the start of the day.

Tomorrow is Sunday, it's different you know,
No need to get up, there is nowhere to go.
I wish it would always be this way,
Then I would like the start of the day.

Christy Matta (13)
Abraham Darby School

THE WAYS OF THE SEA

The sunset was aesthetic, as it shimmered over the sea.
As the gentle swell hid the dangers of the deep.
The changing of the tides were flowing and ebbing,
Relentlessly onto the shore.
The waves seemed to be never resting as they splashed
Against the rocks with an untold force.
But beware, the sea can be turbulent as well as calm.

Matthew Onions (13)
Abraham Darby School

On a Hot Summer's Day

On a hot summer's day,
When all the birds and bees sway.
See people walking in the park,
Then hear dogs begin to bark.

Cats in the sun
And people having fun.
Girls and boys running through the trees,
Playing games like cops and thieves.

Sunbathing people getting a tan
Children chasing the ice cream van
Kids running about
With water guns and hose pipes out.

As the sun sets in
And the light is getting dim
The children and parents run home
Resting for the next day of fun.

Merryn Kelly (13)
Abraham Darby School

Summer Afternoon

I sat on the sandy, sunny beach surrounded by rocks,
I sat and had a delicious drink out of my mom's best crocks,
I started to stare into the brilliant, bright blue sky,
I saw flying seagulls soaring slowly by,
I saw the fish in the swishing sea, swimming round,
I saw the shells shining still in my hand I was proud,
Oh what a delightful summer's afternoon,
I hope I come back again very soon.

Bethany Alcock (13)
Abraham Darby School

MY LIMERICKS

There was a young man from Hortonwood
Who swore he saw Robin Hood
Amongst the tall trees
And the piles of leaves
That's where the young man saw Robin Hood.

There was a young man from Blackpool
Who totally hated school
He hated the tests
So he took a long rest
That silly young man from Blackpool.

Melissa Bailey (11)
Abraham Darby School

KITTENS AND THEIR MOM

Look how the mother looks
after her kittens
watching them play
with little mittens.
She watches out for them
like chocolate and sweets
then dinner comes
with lots of meats.
Then strangers come
and she watches her kittens
being taken away
and she hopes to see them
another day.

Laura Markland (13)
Abraham Darby School

SPIDERS

He deadly and big to all insects around,
He'll take one snip and suck up the melted mound.
He looks at you with all eight of his devilish eyes
And grips your skin with those eight furry legs,
He, is a tarantula.

She's as small as a child's nail,
She's as nimble and quick as light itself.
She'll bite into you with her two long fangs
And make your whole body flop to the ground.
She is all black with a red spot on her back,
She, is a black widow.

Joseph Clutton (12)
Abraham Darby School

JACK THE GINGER STRIPY CAT

Jack the ginger stripy cat
Lazy and fat, curled up in a ball,
Shake the biscuits,
Open the tin,
He raises one eye and slowly walks in.
A munch and a crunch
Then dinner's all gone,
He finds a nice spot
And lies in the sun.

Sian Jones (12)
Abraham Darby School

I Thought . . .

I thought you were my boyfriend,
I thought you said you loved me,
I thought I could love you back,
I thought I could hold you in my arms,
I though you were special,
I thought I could understand you,
I thought love could last forever,
I thought I had someone to talk to,
I thought you were a good listener,
    I thought wrong!

Shelly Ashman (12)
Abraham Darby School

New York's Pork

There was a young man from New York
Who decided to eat some tender pork
He choked on the bone
And he cried and he moaned
That silly young man from New York.

James Hill (11)
Abraham Darby School

The Sweet Sea

The sea is like an eye,
Forever deep and blue.
The sea is like our love,
Forever like me and you.

The sea is like a candle,
Shining with all the light.
The sea is like a star,
Twinkling in the night.

The sea is like a blanket,
Covering all of the fish.
The sea is like a crater,
Like a big, wide ocean dish.

The sea is like a person,
Hiding its true feelings.
The sea is like a house,
The walls, doors and the ceiling.

Stephanie Leach (13)
Abraham Darby School

SUMMER DAYS

Summer air,
Kites fly,
Birdies in the
Blue sky.

Long days
In the sun,
Children play,
Having fun.

Barbecues in the night,
Sausages and steak.
Hot coals, get too close,
Cook gets angry needs a break.

Water fights
All day through.
I love the summer,
Don't you too?

Amy Fletcher
Abraham Darby School

SEASONS

Months and months go round and round,
 these are the seasons to be found.
Mother Nature casts her spell,
 so all living things will do well.
Tulips standing up so tall,
 ivy climbing up the wall.
Lambs are ready to be born,
 maybe they'll be here by dawn.
Lazy lily ready in bloom,
 too many daisies have taken up room.
Sunny days and light winds blow,
 so all the plants begin to grow.
Cornfields sway side to side,
 as we're here for the ride.
Twisting, twirling to the ground,
 the leaves fall without a sound.
Yellow, red, green and brown,
 as they fall down and down.
The wind is giving a gentle blow,
 causing the trees to sway to and fro.
Children searching all around,
 loads of conkers to be found.
The icy snow falls to your feet,
 like a carpet, is the sleet.
As winter's here,
 the nights draw near.
The glistening snow lies on the trees,
 no animals around, not even bees.
A sheet of white lies on the ground,
 covering everything without a sound.

Emma Fletcher (13)
Abraham Darby School

A TOUR OF PARIS

A trip round the Palace of Versailles
Trees and fountains reach way up high
Rosebuds smell sweet in the air
Wander around without a care.
Chandeliers drip diamonds and light
Regal surroundings, a magnificent sight
Gilded rooms, glowing gold
Draped velvet, no unwanted fold.

Designer names on fashionable things
Beautiful clothes and sparkling rings.
Paris couldn't be much better
Shopping in the city centre.
Paris is a shopper's delight
Stay to see the lights at night
Walking down the Champs Élyées
A wonderful time to spend as you please.

At sunset the riverboat will glide
Have a candlelit meal inside
The day is drawing to its close
The band starts 'La Vie en Rose'
Out of the window a wonderful view
Shining and sparkling like brand new
The Eiffel Tower lit up against the sky
To Paris you won't want to say goodbye.

Amelia McCabe (11)
Charlton School

FAIRY TALE - MODERN POEM - MOUSE!

Once upon a time,
There was a man with a house,
It was large and fine,
Except for a big white mouse.
The man was very afraid
And didn't know what to do,
No progress was being made,
So he stood on a stool.
He cried out for help,
Hoping someone would come,
As his hopes started to melt,
He was surely having no fun.
But suddenly appeared,
A woman out of the blue,
There was nothing she feared
And nothing she couldn't do.
More beautiful than a unicorn,
On a beautiful summer's day,
A Hoover was her thought
And she sucked the mouse away.
His hair was sleek and shiny,
Her skin was pure as a dove,
Now they shared something mighty,
The powerful thing called love.
But then there was a tragedy,
Nothing known by this bloke,
The pain stung worse than a bee,
For a nail she had broke.
Her eyes were no longer a periwinkle-blue,
But a cold, dark grey,
She cried, 'This is all thanks to you,
I shall haunt you from this day!'

A witch she had become,
In this large, fine house,
'I shall chase you for what you've done,'
And she turned into a large white mouse.

Melissa Grindrod (15)
Madeley Court School

A GHOST

You are the wind's whistle
You are a wispy grey
You are the night's servant
You are a field's fog
You are a student of Mrs Perrins
You are as tall as a door frame
You are a ghost.

Kirk Smith (12)
Madeley Court School

MY DOG

My dog is as soft as a brush
And as lazy as a bed
Eats pies like there's no tomorrow
Eats toffees like a kid
As dark as a shadow
As bright as a light
His name is Billy.

Daniel Sherry (13)
Madeley Court School

BY THE FIRE

The old, worn boots lay by his side,
Choked in mud, the laces tied.

A handkerchief tucked in his jacket,
A tear-stained rag, deep in a pocket.

His over used pipe, once warm, now cold,
A photograph of the farm he sold.

A jumble of keys, stiff on his chest,
Spoiling his Sunday best.

But sitting, open on his lap,
A headline, 'Foot-and-mouth strikes back'.

Athena Lill (15)
Madeley Court School

THE MOON

The moon is a big piece of cheese
floating over the water.

It is a puddle of white paint
spreading in the sky.

It is a white thumbprint
on a black sheet of paper.

It is a white beach ball
twisting in the sky.

It is a white chocolate button
sailing in the sea.

Georgina Kilford (12)
Madeley Court School

MIDNIGHT SKY

M y window which I look out of every night
I nside there's reflection from the moonlit night.
D awning onto me, the misty feeling.
N ow tonight the sky you have to believe in.
I cicles hovering across the shades of blue.
G littering, gleaming, all so new.
H ighland scenery completely the sky.
T he stars peering down onto us, so bright.

S o that's what I whispered one night,
K nowing the moon can glow so bright.
Y ou'll see some night . . .

Nicola Little (13)
Madeley Court School

LOST IN THE WOODS

The old remains of brand new shoes,
Inside a bag he never used.

A broken chain with rusting parts,
Unmendable like broken hearts.

A circle of the finest lace,
Thrust upon his sleeping face.

A special picture of a friend,
Entwined with rope they'd bought to lend.

Strangled roses in a bunch,
Hiding evidence of a punch.

Around his neck were colours to mourn,
Black for sadness, red for scorn.

Elizabeth Smith (15)
Madeley Court School

A GHOST

You are grey like a cold, rainy day.
You are the howling wind on a dark night.
You are like the graveyard when someone has just been buried.
You are like the forest in the black of night.
You are the villain on Channel Four.
You are a *ghost!*

Sarah Morris (12)
Madeley Court School

YOU ARE ...

You are silence on a dark night
You are an electric cut in thunder and lightning
You are a mist coming from under the door
You are cats' eyes in the middle of a foggy field
You are a crash when you're all on your own
You are a rattling key in the rusty lock
You are a *ghost!*

Lauren Jones (12)
Madeley Court School

THE GHOST!

You are as white as a white board.
You are as grey as a storm.
You are as dull as a rainy day.
You are as quiet as a mouse.
You are as slow as a snail.
You are almost see-through.

You are a ghost ...

Sammy Blake (12)
Madeley Court School

YOU ARE ...

You are a creaky door opening at night,
You are a full moon on Hallowe'en,
You are mist under the door,
You are a scream out of a horror film,
You are the cold in fierce wind,
You are the baby crying in the cradle,
You are music playing,
You are a shadow.

Janine Unwin & Stacey Bevan (12)
Madeley Court School

GHOST

You are cold like ice.
You don't look very nice.
You are like a dim light bulb.
You look like a man.
You are so annoying I want to hit you with a pan.
You smell like mud.
You went through the wall.
You are a *ghost!*

Jason Smith (12)
Madeley Court School

THE MOON

The moon is like a piece of Babybel cheese
floating on the deep blue sea.
It is a Viscount reflecting on the calm blue river.
It is like a baby's face shining down.

Nathan Hammond (13)
Madeley Court School

DEATH

You are the blackness in the dark, gloomy sky.
You are the sadness in a baby's heart.
You are the pain and suffering in a tumble.
You are the moaning in a diseased child.
You are the nightmares of an unknown child.
You are the haunting on All Hallows Eve.
You are the mystery of the soil.
You are the shutting of a coffin.
You are the creaking of old worn stairs.
You are the splinter in a child's finger.
You are the darkest shadow.
You are the dagger in a person's heart.
    You are death.

Kelsey McClean & Stacey Winton (12)
Madeley Court School

HAIKU TERROR POEMS

In the wilderness
come hear the mountain wolves cry
the night will be long.

Just look at my hands
you made them battered and scarred
tears run down my face.

Standing on a cliff
why did my life come to this?
It has been in vain.

Katie Davies (11)
Meole Brace School

AUTUMN

Winter's coming! Winter's coming! Winter's coming!
Cold outside, heating on, fires burning.
The nights draw in, the trees' leaves die, the birds stop singing.
As you trudge to school, in the clearing mist
with the church bells ringing.
The frost bites your fingers, the ice stings your toes,
condensation when you breath.
The Christmas lights go up, the bells start to jingle,
late night shopping starts.
With ten weeks to go the rush starts, Christmas looms,
millions are spent.
Autumn's here! Autumn's here! Autumn's here!

Peter Landers (13)
Meole Brace School

AUTUMN . . .

Autumn is crisp and crunchy.
Leaves fall off the trees,
High up in the air, the birds are leaving
And the clouds roll in to take their place.
Nights are getting colder and days are getting shorter.
Animals are going to hibernate.
Different shades of colour appear,
As if a picture is being painted.
Children playing, laughter fills the air.
It's quiet as if something's going to happen.
Winter's on his way.

Autumn is great!

Kerry Coombes (13)
Meole Brace School

WHAT IS WINTER?

Winter is excitement, fun and laughter,
Warm fires roaring in dim orange light,
Decorations beautifying each and every corner,
Hot chocolate heating from the inside out.

Winter is wearing thick, puffy jackets and wellies,
Reviving frozen fingers by the homely smelling fire,
Finding perfect presents for friends and families.

Winter is carols humming softly in your head,
Walking up the Wrekin on the eve of Christmas Day,
Getting tired and sleepy, then snuggling down in bed.

Winter is dreaming happily of December the twenty-fifth,
Waking bleary-eyed wondering why you are ecstatic,
Then remembering . . .
It's Christmas!

Emily Rayers (12)
Meole Brace School

WINTER . . .

Is short, cold, crisp days of snow and ice,
Wrapped up warm in winter clothes,
Clear skies, icy roads, snowy slopes,
The day as light and bright as a street lamp,
Kids throwing balls of melted snow,
Christimas, a time of celebration, reunion and happiness,
Winter just shines with excitement,
Winter is beautiful.

Edward Ashlin (14)
Meole Brace School

MY POEM ABOUT SUMMER AS I KNOW IT

Summer . . .
Is a time of great happiness and warmth,
Children play merrily upon the lush green grass.
The eyes of the sun watch you,
Her rays swoop down and touch the skin of a human
And brown it slightly.
People dance on soft warm sand,
As waves crash down and consume sandcastles.
The excitement of a holiday builds,
Up as the days pass,
My mum invites her friends over,
For a nice long chat.

Summer is my time of the year,
It is a time of great wonders
And splashes of colours,
But autumn is nearly here.

Melanie Brenner (12)
Meole Brace School

AUTUMN IS LIKE . . .

A rainbow, the leaves, red, yellow,
Brown, purple, mauve and green.
The sunlight, shining through the bare and empty trees.
Crunching, rustling, dry and crisping, dying leaves.
The exploding fruits mellow and all its newborn seeds.
The fruit bursts, popping with golden, warm fullness.
As Christmas draws near and the children cheer
And as the frost begins to show
Oh never forget, I say never forget
Nature's firework display this year!

Sophie Nicholls (12)
Meole Brace School

THE BODY IS A MACHINE

Your body is a machine
Everlasting till you die
Your brain is the boss
It tells you how, when and why

Your heart is like the battery
Pumping power throughout your system
It keeps you alive day and night
But if it beats hard enough just stop and listen

Your eyes are like telescopes
Watching your every move
Some work better than others
Glasses help them improve

Don't abuse your body
It's a very fragile thing
So take good care of it
And what joy it will bring.

John Pugh (11)
Meole Brace School

AUTUMN

Water trickles tamely down gutters,
It's raining cats and dogs,
As the water hits grassy ground
Lakes form in different shapes.

As we look up in the air,
We see berries blushing with only one care,
Leaves above do swirly swoops before reaching ground,
Like planes landing on a runway of green.

They have patterns on them like uniforms on soldiers.
Wind occurs and they are taking off for another flight.
The last lonely leaf lies on the ground,
Not making movement or sound,
Only an echo of nothingness speaks.

Alastair Stewart (13)
Meole Brace School

LIFE

Your life is worth living,
Don't waste it with lies,
Be someone special,
Don't waste any time.

Get going, get moving,
Start living right now,
Get out there, get living,
Before your time's up!

Your life is a seed,
So tend it with care,
You'll regret it one day
If you don't get out there!

If you don't,
Your life will be dull,
Blank with no colours,
Wherever you go.

So come on, get moving,
Don't have a dull life,
Fill it with colours,
With excitement and spice!

Emily Marston (11)
Meole Brace School

YOUR BODY

Your body is like a computer
full of wires, programs and commands.

Your brain would be the hard drive
full of memories and messages.

Your blood is like the power
vital to the machine.

Your veins carry the power
to every place that it's needed.

The heart would be the plug
nothing can work without it.

Your eyes are the screen
that you use to see.

And your organs are the drives
that nobody can work without.

The mouth would be the speakers
that talk for the machine.

Christopher Howard (12)
Meole Brace School

WAR

Death and decay,
Violence and dismay,
The smell of hatred,
Keeping peace at bay,
Nature burning,
The wounded cry,
'God help us!'
What a way to die!

Destruction looming,
Gunfire booming,
Land deforming,
The blazing of fires,
The Devil admires,
All the people cry,
As the last bombs boom,
The poppies bloom,
War is disgusting.

Robert Davies (13)
Meole Brace School

A SMILE

A smile is a disease,
That can spread far and wide,
So when someone gives you a smile
Don't just run and hide.

Pass it on to someone new,
Hopefully they'll do the same,
Maybe it'll come back to you,
Then you'll know that you've done well.

So if you see around,
Someone looking sad or lonely,
Just give them a smile, no sound,
Big or small, long or short.

It doesn't cost a penny,
So you don't have to pay,
But you'll get a good feeling
And maybe they'll give you a smile one day.

Sarah Lawrence (11)
Meole Brace School

AUTUMN

Autumn . . .
is summer growing old,
winter growing young,
the light is fading, the darkness impending,
leaves fly high, swirling around,
natural fireworks leading the way,
soon falling back to where they came.

I'm flying up, the life of autumn,
I am beautiful, I am gold,
everybody likes me,
I am not one to hate,
but there are a few reasons
why I am not brilliant and great.

The crinkles, the crunches,
the greasy school lunches,
the hours of homework,
the strain on the brain,
back to order, everywhere,
I must escape, back to life.

Ahh, that's it, beautiful nature,
a completely unbeatable cure,
those gorgeous colours,
the French carte d'or,
the forests of beauty swirling in winds,
I love autumn . . .
and it loves me!

Robin Kearney (12)
Meole Brace School

WINTER

Winter . . .
is cold, chilly, short days;
makes my whole body numb.
I like winter.
The children's laughter and enjoyment,
the sparkling of the soft, white snow.
I like winter.
Wrapping up in warm clothes,
the Christmas songs
and the children singing carols,
makes Christmas exciting.
I like winter.
The wonderful smell of Christmas dinner
makes my mouth water.
I like winter.
Jack Frost making the green grass white.
I like winter.
The sizzling sausages cooking
on an open fire
on Guy Fawkes' night.
Fireworks making the night sky bright.
I like winter.
Children making snowmen
and having snowball fights.
I like winter.
Opening stockings with excitement,
running down the stairs
to unwrap the presents under the tree.
The wonderful decorations
around the house.
I like winter.

Katie Cooper (14)
Meole Brace School

WINTER

Winter is . . .
Laughter of children whilst opening presents,
Lights dancing dandily on Christmas trees,
Fires burning like a hot summer's day,
Footprints in snow-covered roads.

Carols being sung outside my favourite shops,
Stars illuminating the pitch-black nights,
Snow being flung like catapults
And for bad reasons, brussel sprouts on Christmas Day!

Children wrapped up like birthday presents,
Big wide smiles as they play with toys,
Trucks, vans and all sorts,
They can't wait till next year.

Jake Andrew (13)
Meole Brace School

WINTER . . .

Is short days and long dark nights,
Crisp leaves crunching under small children's feet
And snowballs hurtling towards you
Like round, white bullets.
The ground is covered with
Blankets of snow, silky and soft.
Snowflakes fall all around
And they light up the sky as the dim sun
Catches a glimpse.
Spider's webs are gleaming and shimmering with frost
As the wind whistles through the tree's leaves.
Winter is the spectacular side of nature!

Zoë Harrop (13)
Meole Brace School

DESPAIR

I'm flailing my arms; can't float for much longer
My arms are tiring of their desperate plea.
Days seem too long, just wish I was stronger,
Now the water is gushing, drowning me.
The leers of monsters cackle and haunt me,
I've tried for too long to fend them away.
I'm alone out here; caught in a rough sea,
I'll switch off my pulse, few want me to stay.
I relax my muscles and sink like stone,
The battle was long now I see a light,
I just let all fears ebb with all thoughts of home;
Simply fade away along with the night

But the echoes of threats follow me down

Grasping my limbs till at last I do drown.

Hannah Wilson (14)
Meole Brace School

SPRING

Spring is . . . newborn lambs, bouncing and jumping.
Children playing and eating Easter eggs.
Days lasting longer, as if someone has
switched the light bulbs from the dull winter
to bright spring.
When you sit outside, you can hear children playing,
See flowers growing.
Winter's over and things are warming up.
I like spring!

Ruth E Bliss (14)
Meole Brace School

NEW YORK

N oises, shrill of a mobile, the shouting of people trying to
overcome the sound, it becomes a competition.
E verywhere I look everything seems to be moving, even the
lamp posts seem to sway.
W indows on the skyscrapers, glisten like mirrors as the
workers check their reflection.

Y elling of frustrated drivers so annoyed they are, like
revving rhinos ready to charge.
O thers shopping, spending hundreds for the latest fashion
and trend.
R escue services go past like a lightning flash,
more havoc on the road.
K ing of kingdoms, that's what we dream, knowing nothing is true.
Terrorist attacks destroy our town, nothing seems to be true.

Alexandra Young (13)
Meole Brace School

AUTUMN'S ARRIVED

I pulled back the curtains and saw a golden brown sheet of leaves
which covered the floor below.
As I wondered downstairs I could smell the sweet porridge
but I still went out the front way.
Leaves were crisping and breaking beneath my feet,
birds were chirping, squirrels running and the smell of new dewy grass.
It was like a new world, a new beginning.
It felt like someone was dragging me away from my nice warm
porridge to a new land where animals ruled the land, no houses
and no pollution. You could feel the cool, fresh breeze sway past.
It was autumn, summer was over.

Kelly Redge (13)
Meole Brace School

FLORIDA

Florida is a super place to go,
With its sun and the humidity high.
They're all nice people, no one is your foe
There's always a restaurant to eat a pie.
There are plenty of theme parks to enjoy,
Everything needed is here. Sun, sea and sand
Whatever your age, whether girl or boy,
At the end you'll definitely be tanned.
In the sunshine state, there is much to do.
There are roller coasters and water parks,
Disneyland with Mickey and Goofy too,
With all these things, Florida gets full marks.
One thing wrong is when the hurricanes blow,
Much is wrecked and the winds are hardly slow.

Danny York (13)
Meole Brace School

THE AUTUMN IS COMING

The trees are turning orange and brown,
The leaves are falling on the ground.

The autumn is coming,
The nights are drawing in.

The nights are getting longer,
The days are getting shorter.

The darkness is creeping upon us,
The light is running away from us.

The autumn is coming
And the summer is going.

Chloe Barre (11)
Meole Brace School

TERROR

I'm standing in the shade of the two tall towers,
Standing proud for hours and hours.
Little did we know that they would soon be gone,
America, America hear our song.

The bells go down at the fire headquarters,
People rushing to find their sons and daughters.
The sound of screaming will soon be gone,
America, America hear our song.

The planes of terror went shooting through the sky,
Like a bat out of hell making millions cry.
When did this world go horribly wrong?
America, America hear our song.

Amie Bennett (13)
Meole Brace School

HE'S COMING HOME

I can't believe he's coming home today
I've been waiting for him the whole day
He's coming back from that big place in France
He'll want Mum to clean his clothes and pants
I envied him so much when he was there
But now I really, really do not care
He must have had a lot of watery fun
Teaching and surfing in the nice hot sun
If he had not come home before Thursday
He would have missed his twenty-first birthday
When he leaves after staying here
I won't see him for another whole year
He's probably heading back on the train
Because he's going abroad again.

Tom Ford (13)
Meole Brace School

BEAUTY OF A STAR

As the silver, fluffy clouds float by,
They reveal the bright, twinkling stars.
As beautiful as golden gems,
Like icy jewels shining bright.

The candyfloss clouds swim away
Leaving the dark sky and glimmering stars alone.
Shimmering like a disco ball,
In the black of the silent night.

The gleaming charm gazed down on the world
As the foamy cloud sailed freely through the air
The treasure disappeared like a fish in the sea.

Kirsten Jones (11)
Meole Brace School

MY PURPLE PIT

My metal music deafens the whole street
We're banging our heads to the heavy beat.
The groan of 'Turn that down!' comes from below
It's a small noise with a reply of, 'No!'
I look at my posters, all are a blur,
Black, mixed with some colour, wait and then stir.
As I open the window, light pours in
And fills my purple pit just like a bin.
Around my room are a lot of candles,
I even have a stand for my bangles.
My CD holder is shaped as a cat
And from my ceiling hangs a flying bat
My purple pit is somewhere to abscond,
The real world - a place I'm not too fond.

Emily Davies (13)
Meole Brace School

AMBITION

My ambition is to be a professional footballer,
To play for Villa and England,
To be a strong centre half
And to win the Premier League.
To play in Europe would be my ultimate dream,
To step on Wembley's pitch and hear the crowd roar,
The crowd cheering your name,
Turn into one of the supporters' favourites,
The feeling would be awesome.
Hoping my family would be proud of me,
The nerves and adrenaline pumping,
Not knowing if I'll make a mistake on my debut,
To go to the World Cup,
Score the winner in a FA Cup Final,
However, I suppose I might have to settle for playing for Wolves.

Scott Bailey (13)
Meole Brace School

MY BEST FRIEND . . . SUMMER

Summer's wonderful.
She's bright, full of laughter, bubbly, pretty and a great friend.
She's the sort of person you'd want to cheer you up when you're sad.
When you're with her, there's never a dull moment:
Barbecues, water fights, holidays and paddling pools.
She's my idol, I look up to her for everything:
Which clothes to wear and where to go.
When I'm with her, the sun's always out.
Her garden's full of flowers,
She's my best friend.

Hannah Calderbank (13)
Meole Brace School

ST IVES

While printed walls, smells of salt and of sea,
Fisherman's boats line the beautiful quay.
Seagulls sweep and swoop over granite crags,
Fluttering, floating like white linen rags.
Wavy from the vast ocean crash on the sands,
White from drifts gently across the slim bands.
The relaxed feeling of the busy place,
Sweet shops opening their doors to slow pace,
Aromas wafting through the awakening town.
Tropical, kaleidoscopic climate,
Orange Mediterranean climate.
White painted walls, smells of salt and of sea.
Fisherman's boats line the beautiful quay.
Deep blue Mediterranean Sea.

Joshua Pharo (13)
Meole Brace School

STORMY BAY

Large brick castle on the cliff,
Roaring tides and ships adrift,
Sharpened rocks in a monster's mouth,
Jagged teeth always pointing south.

Sailors hate that stormy bay
Darkened waters in a shallow place.
Many a man has been departed,
From his ship and into darkness.

My house looks upon the wreckages
Drowned in seaweed, torn on sharp edges.
Not much left now, just some timber,
Calm seas now until next winter.

David Humphreys (13)
Meole Brace School

HAIKU POETRY

The girl with trousers
is a tomboy who likes boys
playing on skateboards.

The teacher's talking
about haiku poetry
'Now write one yourself.'

Cat's time for dinner
come in for food, Isabell.
The cat's bowl is empty.

The sky is cloudy
we're writing haiku poems.
After we're playing.

I'm writing poems
listening to the teacher,
imagining things.

The dog needs a wash
he's running around the house
finally he's clean.

The plants are outside,
towering above the window
yellow and green leaves.

Dannielle Tennant (11)
Meole Brace School

SUMMER, SUMMER, SUMMER IS HERE

Summer has arrived,
The plants are turning green,
The sun is shining brightly
Over the trickling stream.

Ice lollies melting in my hand,
My skin is burning hot,
My feet are sinking in the sand,
Flowers blooming in their pots.

Summer has arrived!

Shariel Page (13)
Meole Brace School

FITNESS

Your body's a machine,
There's a few things to do,
How to keep fit.
I'll tell you!

Try to keep healthy,
You'll also be fit.
You can do different things,
Just put your mind to it.

Don't give up trying,
It may be rough,
Keep on going,
When it gets tough.

The jogging, the running,
The rowing, the weights,
Cycle to work,
You won't be late!

Now you're healthy,
You're really fit,
Keep going, keep trying,
You've mastered it.

Natalie Fisher (12)
Meole Brace School

LIFE

The part of my life,
Where your face is a knife,
Sharp, dangerous with a reflection of fear,
Nowhere to want no one near.

Feeling neglected and alone in sorrow,
Wanting there to be no tomorrow.
Painting anger all over the walls,
Crying and screaming, not caring at all.

If the world was like it was today,
There wouldn't be cursing or crying each day.
Today everyone's alive and speeding through life
And we have blunted the sharpest knife.

The solution to life is to be happy not sad,
To be good to yourself and not be bad.
Don't turn to violence hate or drugs,
If so then just pull out the plug!

Ella Wellings (13)
Meole Brace School

WINTER, WINTER

Winter, winter,
Shining bright
In the mists of the night.
Chilly December arrives each year,
Blazing fire, Christmas is near.

Winter, winter,
Shining bright,
Children outside having snowball fights.
Opening presents on Christmas Day,
I know soon winter will go away.

But for now I say:
Winter, winter,
You are the best,
Shining bright like a grateful guest.

Rachel Price (12)
Meole Brace School

FLIGHT

Flight, a man's domination of life and soul,
To overcome the might of the gravitational black hole.

Soaring through the skies, swooping and gliding,
The birds of Earth, magnificent creatures,
A role model for all men and women
With spectacular features in spring, autumn, summer or winter.

Planes are a source of amazement and great history,
From the flimsy, floppy Wright brothers' plane,
To the speedy, stylish jets of today.

The G-force is a man's best friend from flight to flight.
It feels as if you've been hit by a train.
The bang and the roar of the engine's fast, furious, flutter
To the silent glider as quiet as a squirrel.

The fantastic views from 3,000ft,
Looking down on the lovely countryside and different fields,
As if all the fields were sewn together in one big quilt.

They defend our spectacular country from peace to war,
Bearing the frontline attack of the enemy's mighty charge.

We always forget how important planes are,
But next time you see a plane, think,
That plane has the marvel of flight.

Darren Edwards (12)
Meole Brace School

SMILE

On your face you have a mouth,
Make it wriggle,
Make it pout,
Make it squiggle.

Help it glow,
Because it's a light,
Put it on show,
Make it smile right!

You can make it shine,
Colour it red,
Now it looks like wine.
It's the prettiest thing on your face.

In the dark, while you sleep,
Your lips become dry
And you don't weep,
Not even a tear drips from your eye.

Having a smile
Can be quiet or loud,
Not in a book or file,
But on your face where it beams out proud.

Nicola Morgan (12)
Meole Brace School

A SCHOOL DAY

Writing and running
Skipping, thinking and watching too
Is a school day for me.

Jade Jones (11)
Meole Brace School

A NEWBORN SEED

A newborn baby,
Is just like a seed,
You are the mother,
She needs you to feed.

The flower starting to move about,
Every day learning a new thing,
Learning to talk
And even to sing.

She begins to bloom,
You're watching her leave home,
Smelling like perfume,
As she begins to roam.

Losing her colourful petals,
As she begins to strain,
Gradually dying,
In a lot of pain.

Hayley Scott (12)
Meole Brace School

SUMMER IS

Light and vibrant
Happy and hot
With showers of flowers
And shady spots
With lots to drink
It makes you think
What a fuss we make
Over this wondrous thing.

Sean Martin (13)
Meole Brace School

SEASONS

S   heep grazing in the field.
P   eople preparing picnic lunches.
R   unning round, having fun.
I   n the garden daffodils grow.
N   ewborn lambs;
G   rowing into adult sheep.

S   un shining brightly;
U   nder the hot sky I sit;
M   ild breeze in my face;
M   y body's being burnt but still I sit,
E   verybody else had sense to seek, protection from the
R   ays of the hot summer sun.

A   fter summer comes the autumn;
U   nder the trees which leaves have fallen.
T   he days grow short, the nights grow long,
U   nfamiliar surroundings start to make sense,
M   onday, Tuesday, Wednesday, the countdown till winter.
N   ovember's here, my birthday's near.

W   inter's now here, the sleet and the snow,
I   nside it's warm, outside it's cold.
N   ovember seems so long ago.
T   he sun is shining yet still it's cold,
E   verything white and clean with snow.
R   emember the year that seemed to go so slow.

Natasha Hall (11)
Meole Brace School

THE JUMP

1, 2, 3 . . .
Go!
My heart beats! This is it!
No going back, off the down ramp
People rise ahead of me
I can feel the sweat rolling down my face
The cold spring day makes my face cold and dry
Tears form where the wind whipped me
Team spirit. Remember team spirit!
It was no use, I was in this race by myself.

13, 12, 11 . . .
I am eleventh, only ten ahead
My heart leaps like a dog catching a ball
My bike feels rough,
I ride but it isn't the same
No one ahead
10, 9, 8, 7 . . . my bike feels like it has square wheels
My hands rumble on my bars like a mobile phone
6, 5, 4, 3, 2 . . .
The trees seem to point at me and laugh
Then I see it, the last drop off, 12 foot across
The person was just ahead . . .
Whoosh! The finish line
Victory would be mine
The person in front snapped his handle bars
I smelt an earthy smell
Yes! I had just won it for Fox Racing 2003.

Billy Church (13)
Meole Brace School

TROUBLE

I was in trouble,
I didn't know what to do.
So I took my dad's word,
And told them the truth.

Out of the frying pan and into the fire,
The trouble was getting worse.
I was burning rubber,
Just like a tyre.

I finally found out,
That telling the truth isn't always a good thing,
Because the grass isn't always greener on the other side.

I never took my dad's advice again,
Because the truth isn't sometimes what you think.

Charlie Ashton (11)
Meole Brace School

ABOUT ME

PeaCeful
HeLpful
HAppy
KInd
ClaiRe
SlEepy

Owen
Working
QuiEt
ThiNking

Claire Owen (11)
Meole Brace School

24 HOURS

When murky darkness quickly closes in
The animals begin to make a din.
The creepy-crawlies looking out at night,
Strange noises made by creatures out of sight.
The wind winding and howling through the trees,
Leaves scattered around by a sudden breeze.
The hooting of an owl through the night's sky
And the fox, who's stealing food on the sly!
The bright morning sunshine makes me smile.
Out of the window I can see for a mile.
The funnily shaped clouds floating very high,
It's hard to concentrate but I will try.
The brightly coloured rainbow in an arc,
After school I'll ride my bike to the park.
I'll have my tea at six cos my mum said,
Just past ten o'clock I'll go to bed.

Alex Cameron (13)
Meole Brace School

WINTER . . .

Is my favourite season,
Because everyone is happy,
People sing and dance
Until they're bursting with laughter.
They pull crackers and wear paper hats
When Christmas comes.
It seems as though the trees are being eaten,
As the snow crawls up higher and higher,
Thicker and thicker,
Until it's really deep.
Winter is my favourite season.

Robert Griffiths (13)
Meole Brace School

THE BEACH, SUMMER AND WINTER

Golden beaches stretch, far as I can see,
The light blue sea shimmers in the sunlight,
Adults sit down sipping at their warm tea,
Children attempt to fly their big red kites,
A small fishing boat returns with its catch,
People swim and splash to their heart's content,
Some boys run round and have a football match,
A man advertises deckchairs to rent,
Seagulls circle looking for bits of food,
A man lands a fish on the jagged rocks,
Sitting on the cold beach, weather been rude,
Waves crash, rain pours, wind blows over the docks,
Empty beaches, seafront shops are all shut,
Waves hit rocks like a nut cracker cracking nuts.

Ed Mainwaring (13)
Meole Brace School

SUMMER . . .

Is warm and beautiful,
It's long, bright, sunny days,
Time off school to spend on holiday,
Crashing waves on the warm beach sand,
Building huge, great palace sandcastles,
Fresh green grass on garden lawns
And the bright green leaves on the overhanging trees,
Barbecues in the garden heat,
Happiness all around,
Summer is great!

Ruby Honnor (12)
Meole Brace School

JAMAICA

They have big dreadlocks and large fuzzy hairs,
They raise animals and grow nice palm trees,
Jamaican people grow the nicest pears,
They have a cool accent and always please.
Bobsleigh is a favourite sport to them all,
Although they will never have any snow,
The hot summer days and not a football.
A place that I'd really like to go to.
Sunny island, so very far away,
Bright and tropical Caribbean sea,
Home of the Rasta, birthplace of reggae
And not least the legend that is Marley.
You have to go home sometime, it's a shame
And England isn't the same, it's so lame!

Sean Willis (13)
Meole Brace School

WINTER . . .

Is icicles formed
On cold window ledges,
Frost-bitten plants withered and old,
The long lonesome evenings and
The descending darkness
On cold December nights.
Bleak lonely mornings
As if no life is there
Is the cold, true meaning of
Winter.

Claudette C Williamson (13)
Meole Brace School

THE DREAM

The trees stand tall as blue as a bluebell,
The grey grass glittering with dew droplets,
Down a golden path I tumbled and fell,
As I stood up a white rabbit I met.
Light turned to darkness, the sun disappeared,
Shadows of darkness I could only see,
Then in a dark corner something appeared,
Ghouls, ghosts and goblins terrifying me.
Screams from the forest were heard from afar,
This scary world where I wished not to be,
I looked to the sky and saw the first star,
I shut my eyes tight so I could not see.
Suddenly I awoke, sweat down my head,
Then I realised I was still in bed.

Lucy Alexander (13)
Meole Brace School

A WINTER DAY

Snow falls, fluttering down like feathers
As fluffy as cotton wool and glistening
Like diamonds in the winter sun.
As I walk, the flakes of snow
Crunch with each clomping footstep.
Clomp! Crunch! Clomp!
The robin hops from bird feeder to bird feeder,
Looking for its lunch,
Whistling its winter melody.

Red berries bloom on the holly,
The robin singing its tune flies past,
Plucking a berry for its tea.
As I fight the cold winter winds,
I look forward to sipping my hot chocolate and
Gazing into the picture-filled flame pit of my fireplace,
Remember the fun I've had today.
I can't wait for tomorrow!

Tom Williams (13)
Meole Brace School

HOME

There is just one place to be in the world!
When you're away, you're looking to get back,
Back home! Even just to tease my brother Jack.
You can laugh, talk, even crawl over an old sack.
My home makes me feel free like an old tree,
Relaxing! Being lazy, drinking tea.
When I'm at home, I feel safe as a bird,
Snug in its nest, safe from all of harm's reach.

My garden is a place out of the way,
I can be quiet, or I can have fun
And I like playing football in the sun.
My garden is great, so what's more to say.

My home and my garden are the best!
And I will not swap them for any other nest.

Tom Law (13)
Meole Brace School

SCHOOL

Children in their droves flock towards the gates
Marching like soldiers going to battle
A blatant bell rings and so ends the wait
As people flock through small doors like cattle.
The teacher enters and children salute
As the slow daunting maths lesson begins.
Like a wise owl the teacher does hoot
And as the class ends, the pupils all grin.
The day nearly over, spirits are high
The sun beaming on freedom all around,
A final bell rings and all say goodbye
As the last few footsteps finally sound.
No more detentions, the weekend is here,
Sadly my diary isn't clear.

Fern Owen (14)
Meole Brace School

JUNGLE

Eyes everywhere, as you creep around,
Snakes slithering across the ground.
Droplets, draped from elephant leaves
Damp, travelling through the breeze.
Humidity swarming in the air,
Mosquitoes nestling in your hair.
Tiger, watching, closely, coldly,
Follows, stalking slowly, boldly.
Cobra hissing, loud and shrill,
Poison, deadly to shock, to kill.
Darkness sweeps through the skies
Although it sleeps, the jungle cries.

Emma Hartley (12)
Meole Brace School

THE UNICORN

The strange mythical beast stood before me,
Its white form pure against the setting sun,
I sat looking down from high in the tree,
His eyes greeted mine and we became one.

I climbed back down from my place up so high,
The sun felt so warm against my cool skin,
Crossed the wet grass like tears I cry,
I looked forward, my spirit jumped within.

When I reached him, the beast knelt before me,
I moved onto its beautiful white back,
Our minds spoke telepathically,
No unpleasant whip did I need to crack.
And as I remember that night-time show,
To that peaceful dream I wish I could go.

Rosanna Urwick (14)
Meole Brace School

OCTOBER 31ST

October 31st, don't go outside!
There are witches with their broomsticks,
Hovering in the moonlit sky.

Costumed children running in the street,
You'd better watch out,
There's nowhere to hide.

Creepy shadows guarding the dark corners,
They will give you a fright.
October 31st, don't go outside!

Louise Turner (13)
Meole Brace School

WORDS

As a young baby,
your words just don't come out,
you just make noises.

You do also point
but your mum can't understand
your secret language.

As you grow older
you can say short words like *mum*
and maybe *some*.

When you grow to three
you can almost talk properly
like your friends.

Then you get clever
and like to show your words off,
competing like a game.

Joseph Ruxton
Meole Brace School

BARN OWL

As the golden sun sets
and night starts to fall,
he will soar from his barn,
with a hooting call.

He's blinking and winking,
his great big eyes,
they're as big as the moon,
that hangs in the skies.

His feathers are pale and white,
with a hint of gold,
they keep him so warm,
when the weather's cold.

There's no rustle of wings,
he makes not a sound,
as he flies
around and around.

Ani Gallagher-Walker (11)
Meole Brace School

MY WINTER

Autumn's gone, winter's here,
Birthdays and Christmas, drawing near.
Crackling fires burning bright,
In the shadows of the night.

Christmas shopping in the town,
As my presents get bigger, my money goes down.
Snow falling all around me,
Family and friends all surround me.

My birthday has gone,
But we're nearly upon
Christmas Day -
Only one day away.

Christmas Day is finally here
My grandad's in the corner, drinking beer.
After our meal, we all have a rest,
This season is truly the best.

Claire Macklin (12)
Meole Brace School

QUERIES OF LIFE

Whither and die, is what all life must do;
The human from birth and the plant from seed.
Even to one's greatness does death pay no heed,
For you'll know the time; when death comes to you.
It seems but a second as life passes by.
The evil, the good, the brave and unworthy,
Will all be flung down; there's no mercy for thee.
What difference is man, is man from the fly?
Is life freedom? Or is life imprisonment?
Is there a place on to which all will pass?
Does it depend on deeds? Does it depend on class?
Does it not matter? Queries solv'd in a moment.
Man's days are numbered and the clock does chime.
There must be a way, we can defeat time!

Sam Stone (13)
Meole Brace School

SUMMER

Green grass swaying to and fro,
Tiny little insects being heard by smiling faces,
An outburst of bright colours peacefully bathing in the warmth,
Ice lollies melting onto your hands,
Sunflowers twinkling beautifully underneath the glittering sun,
Your friends; dancing like dragonflies over still, glistening waters,
The fresh summer's breeze,
Lets you go on with pressures eased!

Jessica Sanders (13)
Meole Brace School

AUTUMN

Autumn is here,
Let's shout hip-hip-hooray,
Here's what I see,
Day by day.

Trees alight
Like bonfires in the night,
Leaves falling,
Nature is calling.

It is getting colder,
Frost sleeps on the ground.
It is getting darker
As the seasons turn around.

Crunching, munching,
Leaves fall from above,
Bonfires, fireworks,
It's autumn I love.

Andrew Kirby (12)
Meole Brace School

AUTUMN

Rustling,
Leaves golden brown,
Twisting and turning, like
Cornflakes spilling into a bowl.
Crunch!

David Seadon (13)
Meole Brace School

My View

The greens, the browns, the yellows and the reds,
Past the meadows and the dead flower heads.
No one else sees it, it's only for me,
As the autumnal leaves float from the tree.
The huge horses heave, the wild rabbits run,
The leaves turn brown for the lack of the sun.
The bare bushes glint in the morning dew,
The tired trees sway and the long grass too.
There are birds who glide and swoop down to eat,
I watch them perform from my comfy seat.
Picturesque, undisturbed this scene exists,
Through the crisp quiet mornings, through the mist.
The greens, the browns, the yellows and the reds,
Past the meadows and the dead flower heads.

James Brett (13)
Meole Brace School

Wretched Beings

As I sit and ponder over my life,
Vivid thoughts run through my bewildered mind,
Obscene figures, should by time never strife,
That special one who to me was so kind,
Wretched beings demand all that is ours,
Eventually they will not deny,
That innocent creature he devours,

Only by mighty God's will shall I die,
'Tis true, we will succeed, we respect rules,
They shall fail miserably, 'tis proven,
They attack us, bent on conquest, stup'd fools,
Intricate patterns of life have been wov'n,
So we wait and hope our cunningness works,
If not then, let it be, what a cruel world!

Mazin Abdelaziz (13)
Meole Brace School

THE BIG MATCH

The roar of the crowd leaps out of the stand
When the home team scores just as they had planned.
When the noise dies down the play will soon start,
The goal scored was just like watching fine art.
Everyone is chanting and shouting
As the wind comes down, the chill is mounting.
When half-time comes, smells of food takes over.
The crowd's noise could be heard from Dover.
The whistle blows, so the half is now started,
Up the ball goes, all the players part.
Soon the away team scores to level things
The name of the scorer was Martin Briggs.
The game has ended as a bit of a mix,
The home fans will say that it was a fix!

David Phillips (14)
Meole Brace School

From My Garden

Sitting on the long grass, slowly I gaze,
Into the horse's field, over the fence,
The two brown horses blissfully graze,
I look to the windmill in the distance,
Its great white sails spin, facing towards me,
Around it huge, towering trees look tiny,
Suddenly a strong wind blows and I see,
No longer do the sails face towards me.
Disappointed, I look yet further on.
Westwards, I see the sun, a beautiful sight,
Setting behind the trees, soon it'll have gone,
But for now, above me glows a red light,
This brilliant wonder does not last long,
Now the birds sleep and stop singing their song.

David Hall (13)
Meole Brace School

The Morning Rush

The birds sing sweetly in the rustling trees,
As the pale morning light bursts in my room.
I stretch, and put my face into the breeze
Drifting from the window; shakes off the gloom.
Oh, how I love this crisp and fresh morning,
I see the sparkling of frosted grass blades
As the cat creeps in the garden, yawning.

The white moon, in clear and bright sunlight fades.
As my family wakes, the rush begins,
Toast burning, kettle's boiling, wild dashing,
Everyone seems to be walking on pins
And Mum wakes to find her best plates smashing.
But what is all this manic racing for?
To get to school, a tiresome, total bore!

Elizabeth Davies (13)
Meole Brace School

LONELINESS

Standing here alone in the dark,
I thought that you'd be here by now.
There's no footsteps on the ground
And no one's trying to find me this time.
I wonder where you are,
If you know just how I feel.
Cos no one likes to be alone
These tears are streaming down my face,
I wish somebody would come take me home.
My whole body aches
And the pain in my heart won't stop.
The winter air is so cold,
But there isn't anyone to keep me warm.
I guess no one likes to be alone.

Stacey Jones (13)
Meole Brace School

THE HUMAN COMPILATION

War is a black blanket,
Warm with blood, abrasive with cold hearts,
Black with death, shrouded with screaming,
Created by our anger and hatred.

Peace is a white light,
Warm with happiness,
Soft with open hearts,
White with life, filled with laughter.

A soldier is a baby full of guilt
Dead babies make his heart cold and dry
He is a pawn in a game no one can win,
With all the lives in purgatory.

A child full of happiness,
With a large, warm heart,
Will grow to flourish, and be all he can be
Standing in a field, the flowers fuel his glee.

Life is the giver of happiness,
It is the beginning of everything,
It is shaped as a mountain range,
With all its up and downs.

Death is the giver of eternal sleep
It is the end of everything,
It is shaped as a rock,
Cold, hard and heavy.

The blanket is covering the light,
The soldier is stalking the child,
Death is following life,
Only we can change this,
Let's make it *right!*

Cameron Rose (13)
Meole Brace School

WINTER

I love winter
it's nearly here.
Sitting by the fire
and drinking lots of beer.
(In my dreams!)

I like sitting by the fire
in the living room,
Wrapping my nan's present
a witch's hat and broom.

Snowball fights and sledging
are really cool.
Even if I end up,
looking like a fool.

The football season
is well under way.
My favourite team Arsenal
are leading the way.

I look forward
to Christmas Day,
when much wanted presents
are coming my way.

Maybe a football shirt,
something I'd like,
CDs, computer games
or even a bike.

I feel sad
when winter ends,
no gifts to receive,
or any to send.

Nick Humphreys (13)
Meole Brace School

MY LOST LOVE

There once was a sun which heated me,
Every night and day I dream of her.
Then she died and never came back to me,
But still the memories linger, and stir.
Now I am thinking of another way.
I would really love to see her again,
You are being silly, some people say,
But what do they know, those women and men?
Who can never understand what pain means!
Or how such suffering can make me feel.
I can now only have you in my dreams,
You know my love for you is always real.
I cannot love anyone, except you.
Did you love me as much as I loved you?

Andrew Stott (13)
Meole Brace School

SONNET

You get them when you are happy or sad,
You get them when you are upset or mad.
Whether or not you want them, they're always there,
They stick to you like glue, they make you care.
They are annoying, always hanging around,
They never get lost, they are always found.
Wherever you go, they will find a place,
They're in your body language, in your face.

At the worst time, they're the last thing you need.
Waiting around like a dog on a lead.
If you have guilt, or have a big problem,
They betray you, hurt you, but that's just them.
Where would we be without these emotions?
They speed through your blood, causing commotion.

Fiona Edwards (13)
Meole Brace School

SCHOOL

I swear this school is driving me insane,
It's torture and it's wearing out my brain.
I sit here for hours, slowly going mad,
All the children around me, look so very sad.
I hate the teacher nagging all the time,
Whilst my concentration starts to decline.
My parents say I'm in this school to learn
But instead my ears are starting to burn!
The time in here moves mind-numbingly slow,
We wait 'til we can leave the room and go.
I don't know how much of this I can stand,
It feels like they've kept me here on remand.
It's okay, the bell has gone, we are free!
But alas, next lesson is geography!

Matthew Coey (13)
Meole Brace School

SUMMERTIME

School's finally over, it's time to have some fun,
Instead of walking slowly, we can skip and run.
A trip to the seaside, swimming in the waves,
Walking up the beach, exploring dreary caves.

Water fights in the garden, with birds' tweeting songs,
An ice cream in the summer heat doesn't last very long.
Buzzing and humming from flying bees,
With the sweet scent of the blossoming trees.

The flowers are in bloom, vibrant and bright,
At 10 o'clock at night, my garden is still light.
Summer's finally here, but not to stay,
So it's best to stay out in the sun for most of the day!

Lauren Shannon (12)
Meole Brace School

MY WONDERFUL PLACE

There is a place, a most wonderful place,
Where the hot summer day is not a race.
Where the sharp grains of sand are a golden brown
And this place is far away from a busy town.
The sea is a glistening tropical blue
And all you can hear is distant cows moo.
The towering cliffs behind the small beach
Only makes it accessible from boats' reach.
There is the occasional seagull's cry,
As it circles round into view of the eye.
Black heads pop up close to the beach's shore.
Silent and still is the seal, not like a lion's roar
And this small place, is a most wonderful place.
Where the hot summer day is not a race.

David Griffiths (13)
Meole Brace School

AUTUMN

Is,
Crayon-coloured leaves and light blustery winds,
The leafy patchwork ground that makes a crunching sound.
Is
Animals gathering food ready for hibernation,
Scuttling around on the cold, damp earth, trying not to be found.
Is,
Bonfires, fireworks and lots of crazy calypso colours,
Children looking happy because Christmas is near.
Is,
The best season of them all,
Called 'fall'.

Mark Young (12)
Meole Brace School

WINTER

Winter . . .
Is short busy days of darkness and cold,
People wrapped up warm, walking along
grey slushy streets.
Frost as white as icing sugar,
Pitted snow beneath dripping icicles,
Ice as misty as the winter mornings.
Inside, houses are blazing with Christmas card colours,
Excited children tucked up beneath cosy covers.
Downstairs, singing and dancing
whilst reminiscing
Crunching and slurping, gulping and chatting
The streets are alive with celebration.
Winter is Jack Frost showing off!
I love winter.

Emily Smith (13)
Meole Brace School

MY WINTER

Blues, whites, long cold nights,
Snow, trees and whirling winds.
Dark colours and snowballs thrown,
Flakes flying as if they're travelling
And fires sparkling.
Last season, celebrations start,
Beautiful high trees like giants standing still,
With lights brightly flashing.
Cosy, delicious and smells so delightful,
Humming, shuddering as cold goes through your body,
Laughter, happiness and family all together,
Icicles flowing, trees flowing,
Leaves falling . . . slowly
And winter
Has begun.

Amy Williams (12)
Meole Brace School

AN INSPIRATION

Far better it is
To dare mighty things,
Than to rank with those poor
Timid souls
Who know neither victory nor defeat.

They say to the strong-hearted,
A dream is not always a dream,
Because sometimes it happens.
No matter who or what you face if you give
One hundred percent, you will always have a
Chance of winning.

It is true to say that death smiles
on all of us
But all a man can do is smile back.
If a man will not die for something
he believes in
He is not fit to be living.

Danny Williams (13)
Meole Brace School

SUMMER

Is my brother moaning it's too hot?
The sun beating down on my neck,
The luscious green grass weeping
Between my sweltering feet.

Cool breeze beneath the trees
Soothing my worn out face.

Summer is my favourite season,
Sun up there, standing high,
Shouting off its heat.

It's like he is the boss and
We have what he has.
He's the boss
And wants to show it.

He's the sun and wants to show it.
He's the boss and proud of it.
The sun is there, always high,
Bright and sunny all the time,
Swimming in the pool all day,
Coming out wrinkly.

Rick Keville (13)
Meole Brace School

SUMMER, SUMMER, SUMMER

The season which everyone loves,
It's lovely to hear the birds and doves,
No scary and creepy dawns
But there are the beautifully cut lawns.
The paddling pool comes out for people,
But no rain - not even a trickle.
Everyone enjoying a peaceful drink,
Sometimes turns out into a terrible fight
As the sun starts to die,
Sooner or later it comes back to fry
Then the barbecues come out all over.
The taste is so nice, it makes your tummy turn over.
Then that's the end of summer
For everyone or other.
Goodbye summer.

Danny Sadd (13)
Meole Brace School

WINTER IS . . .

Crisp and clean and fresh,
Cold toes warming by a blazing log fire,
Skies as white as the ground below
That's covered in crisp and crunchy snow.
Holly hangs by the Christmas tree,
Reddest reds and greenest greens,
Trees like big vanilla ice creams
Standing in the garden, white and sleek.

Emma Thomas (12)
Meole Brace School

THE YEAR

The year is full of magical seasons, weird and wonderful in their
                                                            different ways,
Spring steadily creeping silently round trees
Brings rings of flowers under each delicate footprint
Carries newborn lambs, placing them lightly on the gentle
                                                            green meadow
And fills the air with beautiful birdsong . . . new life.
Summer's sunshine smile spreads the Earth with laughter
Yellow . . . hot sands and calm seas, making the children
                                                            squeal with joy
The Caribbean colours, blend and intermingle with the
                                                            relaxing families
And the sun blazes its heat out for days on end.
But Autumn soon overtakes and spreads the world with her
                                                            golden colours
The reds, golds and oranges look like a blazing fire in the
                                                            darkening sky
In her wake, the trail of leaves she has left, swirls about in the
                                                            gathering breeze
Snow falls, icicles lengthen under rooftops and hail beats down
                                                            on the dark windows.
Winter has arrived, gliding over the shadowed houses below her
The dark nights, the cold winds, the mists and fogs close in, which
                                                            she mixes with her frosty cloak
And then trees appear with lights and decorations, like a
                                                            rainbow picture
Laughter with families and races to the tree on Christmas morning
Turkey dinners and mince pies she delivers and she gathers up
                                                            the snow cloak
For it is time to change again, and this year is gone . . . for good.

Amy Fry (12)
Meole Brace School

WINTER WORRIES

People cold, people grumpy,
I'm listening to the snowflakes falling gently.
Babies crying, mummies whining,
Snow is crunchy,
Ice is smooth,
Decorations up and glowing,
Present buying,
Ladies dining.

Mug of cocoa,
Warm and soothing,
Fires crackling, snowdrops singing,
Eating dinner,
Crying sinner.

Light of life,
Dark of death,
Shouting and
Carol singers.

Matthew Pope (13)
Meole Brace School

WINTER

Winter is a season of coldness,
There's ice and frost and snow,
But there's a place where you can always find warmth,
Next to the fire's glow.

Winter is a season of dullness,
It's dark and misty and grey,
But there are many coloured lights on the Christmas tree
And colourful presents on Christmas Day.

Winter is a season of many great foods,
The taste of roast turkey and sprouts,
There's Christmas pudding for afterwards
And mince pies we can't go without.

There are many different noises at wintertime,
The chirp of the robin on the ground,
The laughter of children playing in the snow
And opening the presents they've found.

Alice Johnson (12)
Meole Brace School

THE STREAM

I sat alone,
Thinking and listening.

The trees are rustling,
Leaves are falling.

Leaves swaying slowly,
Clouds sweeping quickly.

Feelings of happiness
And wishes of everywhere to be in peace.

A stream made of hot iron
As the wind rips into my clothes

And with no time,
Not even to rhyme,

I sat alone,
Thinking and listening.

Romany Nutland (13)
Meole Brace School

THE TEMPEST

The waves crashed on the deserted deck
And the ice shattered on the mast,
The seas swirled down with torrents of water,
Splashing on jagged rocks.

The salty daggers of ice-cold rain
Plunged upon the salty sea,
The dammed deck of the dangerous foe,
Rocked on the roaring brine.

The smell and taste of the salty waste
Jammed their way into our face,
Until there was nothing, but the darkness swirling,
Water hurling and night sky curling.

Then all with one smash, a pitiful splash
As the hardened boat shattered
On rocks that were battered
To the depths of dead man's woe.

Alison Hosker (13)
Meole Brace School

A SUMMER'S DAY

As I think of summer and what lies ahead,
The holidays are here and school is dead.
With thoughts of sport swirling round in my head,
I decide to get up and get out of bed.

I sprint outside, sweltering in the sun,
Panting and puffing as I run.
I start playing with my friends, having fun,
My day of sport has just begun.

It's getting dark after twelve hours of play,
But we carry on anyway.
Eventually, it gets too dim to play,
Our game is finished; what a day!

I say goodbye and depart from my friends,
So I go inside and my long day ends.

Sam Sherwin (12)
Meole Brace School

WINTER

Winters are packed with warm, cosy evenings in front of the fire
And watching long videos that are on hire.
It is lovely to be home, comfortable and warm,
Waiting till summer, till you can sunbathe on the lawn.
Hot meals are awaiting people to eat them, on the kitchen table,
People listening to stories about a baby being born in a stable.

Presents awaiting to be opened by eagerly waiting children,
Huge meals and rich wines served with Stilton,
Friends and families pop in and out all of the time,
Going out and buying excellent food and wine.
Children too gathering around fires,
Toasting marshmallows to their hearts' desires.

Going and looking for conkers under the trees,
People getting ready for the first freeze,
Children sledging down steep hills,
Beautiful Christmas trees filling up window sills.
People waiting for the first few snowflakes to fall,
Children running outside to build snowmen, small and tall,
People staying up at night watching the Christmas telly.

I love winter.

Emma Bailey (13)
Meole Brace School

FRIENDSHIP

Your friendship is a flower.
It blossoms when you have a new friend,
All colours mean a feeling.

Each petal, a different colour,
Yellow is happy,
Dark blue is sad.

One petal says one thing about them,
Loads make a personality.
Once you put all the petals together,
You make a flower.

As your friendship grows,
So does your flower.
As your friendship goes downhill,
Your flower dies.

Don't let your flower die,
Water it with kindness,
Or even grow a new one
And see it blossom again.

Your flower is used by other people
Who turn it into runny honey,
That way, your friendship is stuck together forever.

As you go out,
Your flower grows
Even more flowers.

As you become best friends,
Your flower turns into
One big flower, like a sunflower.

Don't kill your flower,
No matter what.
Just let it grow and grow.

Lizzie Stephens (12)
Meole Brace School

SUMMER

Is a time for:

Doing nothing,
Just lazily listening
To children chattering,
Making as much noise as an agitated beehive.

Lying down,
Smelling barbecues,
Drinking cool drinks
And relaxing through the long, hot days.

Watching plants bloom,
Bursting into their amazing butterfly colours,
Vibrant, swaying as the cool breeze
Caresses their petals.

Coming to life,
Being so busy,
Except me, watching,
Calmed by the activity around me.

Rowan Connolly (13)
Meole Brace School

FREEDOM

Imagine you're a bird,
Free to do what you want,
When you want,
How you want.

Have the wisdom of an owl,
Stay focused,
Concentrate
And learn more.

Be as graceful as a swan,
Take care,
Don't rush,
Be careful.

Be like a dove,
Keep the peace,
Don't argue and fight,
Make friends, don't break them.

Imagine you're a bird
High in the sky,
Enjoy life,
Be free!

Abigail Edwards (12)
Meole Brace School

AUTUMN

When I imagine autumn, I think of . . .
The ground covered with a carpet of leaves.
Golden, red and orange.
A cool breeze ruffling my hair.
Wrapped in nice warm clothes.

Birds flying to faraway lands,
Warm, sunny and bright.
There they stay until the time is right
For them to return, breezy and bright.

Autumn is a great, glorious, gorgeous season!

Rachel Tree (12)
Meole Brace School

BIRTHDAYS

Birthdays are fun, they always are:
Presents, friends and cake,
Not a care in the world,
Not a black cloud in the sky,
For it's my birthday!

Birthdays fill me with joy inside,
Wonder, amazement, anticipation!
The wondrous cake in all its glory,
Soon I will taste its richness.
Anticipation, what's inside,
The bow-tied, sparkling present?
Amazement, just what I wanted!
What an amazing day!

Games, games, wonderful games,
Hide-and-seek and tig,
Who's going to win?
Nobody knows,
It's all good fun in the end.

Birthdays are great!

Ben Hughes (13)
Meole Brace School

SCHOOL-LESS SKIES AHEAD

Happy summer.
I look at the school-less skies
And relax.
Watery summer,
I squeeze into my wetsuit,
Another year.
Sickly summer,
I gaze at hazy camp fires,
Marshmallows gooey in my mouth.
Dry summer,
The sun, the beach, the camping
And the seaweed.
Strange summer.
I swim with relatives in my hand
And ice cream up my nose.
Expensive summer,
Asking for money, burning holes in parents' pockets.
Happy summer,
Forgetting about time,
It's gone before it starts.

Nothing's steady, but I still feel chained.
Soon the summer's gone again.
Walking idly, blurry days,
Soon the year's gone again.
Happy summer,
Forgetting about time,
It's gone before it starts.
School-less skies ahead, the years are being shed.
Soon, we'll all be dead.

Alex Newcombe-Rose (12)
Meole Brace School

WINTER . . .

Is purity and excitement,
Crisp, crunching snow falling from the grey sky,
Woolly hats, cosy duvets, blazing fires, filling you with warmth.
Family together, laughing,
Red robins tweeting and singing songs,
Snowmen with coal eyes and carrot noses,
Smell of fresh pine from the great, green, shiny Christmas tree.
The frosty moon smiling at you from the spectacular starry sky.
Greens, reds, whites, filling rooms,
Little children running around full of wonder,
Dreamy white chocolate, happiness, cosiness.
Winter is magic.

Phoebe Pickard (12)
Meole Brace School

THE FOUR SEASONS

Summer is full of joy,
Dancing, prancing,
Like a young boy.

Autumn's our time for conkers,
Boys and girls going bonkers.

Winter is time for snow,
Having snowball fights
Till they glow.

Spring is time for sun
And to say,
Hello, hot cross bun.

Chris James (14)
Meole Brace School

AUTUMN

Autumn wakes up one morning
And it goes around announcing itself to the world:

Changing leaves' colours
And making them dance,
Like it is a puppet master.
Autumn scares away the swallows.
It shrieks with delight as fireworks boom in the sky.
Pleasure in hearing you squeal,
As it blows cold round your toes.
Autumn laughs at you
As you wait impatiently for Christmas.
She is beautiful and magical,
Like a queen, regal with royal colours of
Red, yellow and orange.
She makes you want to stay in your cosy bed.
She makes the trees stand naked, straggly and bare.
Autumn may not have Christmas, Sun or Easter Eggs,
But she should be respected
For her power and beauty.

Sarah Guthrie (12)
Meole Brace School

SUMMER . . .

Summer is . . . bright and warm, long days,
Going out with my friends all day,
Swimming in the sea,
Having barbecues on warm nights,
Not having any worries on your mind.
With palm trees standing by the beach,
Summer is great!

Ben Humphreys (13)
Meole Brace School

SEASONS

On the beach, in the sun, kites flying high,
Shouts and cries echo through the sunny sky.
The weather is warm, the weather is fair,
Peals of laughter and joy fill warm air.
Butterflies swoop and flutter in the breeze,
Kids running outside, jumping from their knees.
Lollies and ice creams and picnics outside,
The sun is great, cold I cannot abide.
The cold, dreary nights are very close and near,
I try to pretend I have not any fear.
The icy, cold wind, whipping all around,
Leaves fluttering, twirling, fall to the ground.
The seasons keep changing from warm to cold
And they will continue as I grow old.

Naomi Stokes (13)
Meole Brace School

WINTER

Winter is long, cool, calm and crisp.
Silently snow falls wisp by wisp.
Children on sledges, watch them go fast,
The animals migrate for there's no grass.
Winter's a doorway to a new year,
Soon spring will come, don't you fear.
Enjoy this great time with snowmen and holly,
Sit down by warm fires and let's all be jolly.
Snow-tipped trees stand like tall giants,
But the withering flowers fall like dead lions.
White, wintry wonderfulness broken by Christmas lights
Glaring through the darkness, reflecting on the ice.

James Hickson (12)
Meole Brace School

WINTER

Winter's cold, trees are bare,
Windows are frosty in the evening air.
The sky is dark, dull and grey,
Most of the children have gone home for today.
As it gets darker, the sky is colder,
The decorations on houses are much, much bolder.
Christmas is near, just a few days to go,
Children looking out of windows, waiting for snow.
Christmas is here, decorations are up,
Everyone's drinking sherry, filling their cups.
Families come round, say their greetings,
Colleagues at work have Christmas parties, instead of meetings.
Lights are everywhere, bright around the streets,
Husbands carving their Christmas meat.
Groups of choirs are merrily singing,
While church bells for Christmas are happily ringing.
Winter is cold, trees are bare, leaves are rustling in the cold air.
Winter! Winter! A very good season,
Everyone enjoys it, especially Christmas, what a good reason!

Valentina Biuso (13)
Meole Brace School

SWIMMING

I like to splash around in the water,
This means I don't have much time for school.
Training is hard, but sometimes it is easy,
As the saying goes, 'no gain with no pain'.
Racing is scary and nerves get me bad,
Winning's very happy, but losing is sad.
Encouraging is what we all do best,

Our social life is the biggest part.
We meet up at the weekend for races,
Helping people to get the best places.
We go swimming and shopping as best friends,
We go to bowling and cinema in groups.
Swimming is the best way to spend the night,
Even if we're exhausted, what a sight.

Kate Almond (13)
Meole Brace School

WINTER DAY

Bare trees all dressed up in snow,
Looking like the have somewhere special to go.

In front of the open, roaring fire,
Soaking wet clothes get drier and drier.

Snowmen stand alert and straight,
Waiting for the sun to decide their fate.

Lots of children's laughter surrounds,
New toys making strange new sounds.

Turkey, potatoes, treats galore,
Once you start, you want more and more.

Night draws in and it begins to get cold,
Christmas lights bright and bold.

All tucked up, warm in bed,
Time to rest, dream in your head.

Becky Hanlon (12)
Meole Brace School

AUTUMN

The leaves fell, twirling, twisting to the ground
Where they lay, still and crisp.
Sunlight shone through the old tree's tired, painted leaves,
Making the room seem to glow,
Illuminating the walls with reds and yellows.
The garden seemed to be sleeping, getting old,
I could tell this was the end, yet somehow, it still seemed to live.
Bright, vibrant colours shone, like a firework of nature,
As I walked through my garden the dry, fiery leaves
Crunched and crinkled as I stepped on them.
A bonfire blazed merrily at the far end of my garden,
Sending sparkles and flames high into the sky.
Bang, a firework zoomed into the velvet, midnight sky,
Shimmering, dazzling colours burst from its heart.
The fireworks are like autumn, filled with sounds and exciting colours.
I love autumn, it's alive and free!

Katie Green (13)
Meole Brace School

WINTER WONDERS

I love winter because of the snow,
The fights you can have with your sister and bro'.
Winter is great because of snow fights with friends,
Then sitting by the fire as the day ends.

You can build lots of angels and snowmen as well,
Then to the car at the 11 o'clock bell
And as you guide your car into a space,
You get ready to engage in Christmas grace.

Then as you finally sleep after such a long day,
You dream of skiing and riding your sleigh.
Before you know, it becomes Christmas morning,
Running to sibling's room as day is dawning.

Playing with all my favourite new toys
And as we do this making lots of noise.
Looking outside as sleet becomes murky,
Then smiling as Mum brings in the big, fat turkey.

Joe Hosty (12)
Meole Brace School

WINTER SKY

Soft powder trickles down from the sky,
Adding still more to the mass that has covered the Earth,
Trees burdened with their white load smash up,
Out of the hard soil, clawing for warmth.
A lone leaf hangs on, still fighting bravely against wind.
Wind, a child throwing a temper, tearing away the world.
Jagged blue daggers hang down,
Almost poised to strike.
As dark draws near, child wind subsides,
Leaving the white land bare.
As Moon rises,
Silence draws its cloak over the world
And all is still as Moon's light glitters off the snow,
Where the stars scatter over the dark Winter Sky.

Lewis Pollock (12)
Meole Brace School

AUTUMN

Lifeless, scattered leaves lay crisp on the ground,
A sleepless lull lay in the evening mist,
There was no wind, life gave an eerie sound,
Air on the window, condensation kissed.
The acrid smell of the factory waste,
Swept and swirled up into the hazy sky,
Workers hurried along the streets in haste,
Coming home to hear their young children cry.
So cold, so weary, filled with lack of hope,
Fathers paid a pittance, a worn-out life,
Such a hard working life, how can they cope?
The rich keep control, poverty is rife.
Forever autumn in this cruel world,
Will the workers' joy ever be unfurled?

Sarah Beedles (14)
Meole Brace School

WINTER

It is
Frosty, icy mornings
And long, cold, dark nights.
It is
Christmas time with Christmas trees,
Lit up by colourful Christmas lights.

It is
Lots of presents under the tree,
Tied up with a bow.
It is
Very hard to recognise the town
When it's blanketed with snow.

Alice O'Donoghue (12)
Meole Brace School

COW GIRL

If I was a cow girl I'd ride away,
The horses hooves crackling as they rapidly smash against the
                                          hovering grass.
I'd swing my lasso around and around until the calf got dizzy,
My chaps would rub against the horse's stomach as he gallops,
My face would crumble as the wind darted against my swept-back hair,
Tender, juicy meat would be cooked on the burning, red-hot fire,
We'd look up to see the tall, thin, pointed roof of the tepee.
I wish I was a cow girl.

Naomi Scott (11)
Meole Brace School

APRIL

The tulips laughed at the daffodils,
The tulips opened to the sun,
The daffodils bowed to the rain.

The grass cried because it was raining,
The time came for April showers,
In between, the sun was bright.

The cherry blossom whispered to the tree,
Full bloom was the cherry blossom,
The trees were pretty to see.

The lambs cried to the sunbeams,
The lambs went skip, hop and jump,
The sun made the lambs happy.

The Easter chick sniggered at the farmer,
The Easter chick cheeped away,
Laying all our chocolate Easter eggs.

Samantha Williams (11)
The Mary Webb School

A SHE SCARAB

I saw her beetling in the mire,
Her black coat fitted her
Snugly as a leather skin.
Why should such an elegant, well dressed
Lady be so attracted to dung?

I came to Egypt to meet her,
My notebook on my lap,
My camera at my side,
My breath held in expectation
And here she was,
In front of me now.
The one revered by men and kings,
Her fighting spirit scattering lesser creatures.

She was handsome,
Her armour that of a warrior,
So in creation's name,
Why did she leave her offspring
In this smelly situation?

Of course - she is the scarab beetle.

Keri Daniel (12)
The Mary Webb School

THE MOUSE

The mouse, it creeps across the floor,
It worms itself through every crack in the wall.
It runs through every open door,
Especially when the cat is called.
A mouse can be quite small,
Most of them are grey
And ragged down to the core.

The eyes of a mouse are like
The eyes of an eagle watching its prey.
Its creepy, long tail makes you run away.
Some live inside,
Some live in the outdoors,
Some live in cracks in the walls.
If they live in the outdoors,
They make a nest so they can rest.

Leanne Hughes (11)
The Mary Webb School

THE LEOPARD

The leopard lounges lazily in the treetops of the African savannah,
Her eyes shimmer in the dark like the headlamps of a car,
Her honey fur is splattered with coffee-coloured splodges,
It's as if she has a bad case of measles.
Hidden in her soft, cushiony pads, lie a set of razor-sharp claws,
Ready to spring out like a set of butchers' knives.

Her twitching ears move around sensing her prey,
Like a satellite dish waiting for a signal.
She moves, sleekly and silently creeping up on the victim.
Finally, her sabre-like teeth sink into her prize,
Ripping the meat from the bones.

Underneath her pretty pussycat looks,
She is hiding a ferocious feline
That can only growl aggressively and not purr affectionately.
You can't say that her bark is worse than her bite,
Because her bite is worse than her growl.

She slinks back to her treetop bunk
To overlook her sun-setting savannah.

Claire Vernon (11)
The Mary Webb School

THE BEE

The bee is yellow with black stripes,
It stings with an aggressive bite.
It flies around buzzing in a charge,
Perfect and spotless.
Hundreds and thousands glide in the sky,
Swooping down on every side,
Swarming along to gather the nectar,
Chewing and pre-digesting it.
The honey is in the honeycombs,
For the hard work they do.
The hexagon shape is a familiar view.
I watch with delight,
They circle around the flowers,
At night-time the flowers close,
So the bee rests till the next day.
It is the only insect that can make honey.
The bee is an experienced insect,
It works tremendously fast,
The honey is pure,
We are lucky to have such an insect,
The bee,
It flies around buzzing in a charge,
Hundreds and thousands glide in the sky.
The bee.

Alex Capewell (11)
The Mary Webb School

MARCH

Hooray, she's here bringing joy to the world,
A hobbling hunchback nobody can understand.
Her dusky gown sways in the spring breeze,
One pale, battered hand reaches for a handful of seeds.

Frayed is her hair which swims in a gust,
Her bloodshot eyes catch a glimpse of the earliest snowdrop.
A gentle, croaky voice slithers out of her chapped lips,
'I'm here, here to bring spring to the valleys,'
She whispers as she lets out a smile.

Emily Roberts (11)
The Mary Webb School

A HUGE CREATURE

It's the gentle giant of the jungle,
Big and strong, this huge grey animal
With its big, flapping ears,
It's long, swinging trunk
And brilliant white ivory tusks.
He marches through the hot jungle sun,
All day long.
He searches for water to cool him down,
His hot, dry, wrinkly skin,
He wants to bathe and feel cool,
But it's so hot.
He feels tired plodding along,
Minding his own business,
The ground rumbling and quivering
Beneath his huge feet.
Animals scatter around him,
They climb trees to get out of his way.
He means them no harm,
He eats the leaves from the trees.
Finally he finds his drinking hole,
The one he found last year.
He knew it was there all along,
Because an elephant never forgets.

Luanne Bellis (11)
The Mary Webb School

DECEMBER

Serene and cool as a winter's day,
She covers autumn with a blanket of frost,
Her sapphire eyes gaze around
As she observes the snow on which she stands.
One slender hand gracefully extends a mantle of ice,
Her shimmering lips allow the merest of whispers to escape,
The slim body floats with the elegance of an angel,
She glistens in the sunlight as she drifts in the cold air.
Her lips are as red as berries
And her hair glistens as the frost on the branches of the trees.
Faintly she hears the ring of the church bells in the distance,
She watches families gathering at the church,
While others play excitedly in the snow.
Her ears sense the first sound of a reindeer,
Quietly she withdraws from the landscape for another year.

Lucy Price (11)
The Mary Webb School

WOLF

Sleek and smooth his coat shimmers
In the clear moonlight.
Rough and shaggy, his mane ripples in
The icy breeze that blows over his shoulders.
Large and clumsy feet are placed
Precisely on the craggy ledge.
Poised and standing proud, his warm breath
Puffs out clouds from his nostrils.
With a twinkle in his eye and snarling of his lips,
The wolf throws his head back and howls.
Aahoow!

Sally Poole (11)
The Mary Webb School

LEOPARD

The orange sun rises in the sky,
With the heat of the morning, the clouds rise high.
The leopard wakes up, stretching his paws,
Yawning tiredly and showing his claws.

He wakes up his family in the early morn,
His wife and his sons, his newly born,
Then he goes out hunting in the wild,
With the clouds rolling high, but the weather mild.

But there's a hint in the air of danger it seems,
The red is too dark in the sunlight's beams.
Then the cry of a leopard pierces the day,
Cutting as a knife, never to go away.

The leopard runs as the wind back to his den,
Then he recognises the smell, the smell of men.
Then there he spots it, the glint of a gun,
He jumps on the men, the battle yet to be won.

Then the lead of the gun penetrates his flesh
And he falls to the ground with a mighty crash,
But the leopard bit and tore with his jaws,
Gnashing his teeth and showing his claws.

The men ran away, they feared him badly
And the leopard's family looked at him gladly,
Late that night when all was dark
And the last song had been sung by the lark.

The leopard looked up to show his jaws,
Tossed his head, looked up and roared,
There he died, battered with scars,
But he still remains with us up in the stars.

Emma Marshall (11)
The Mary Webb School

PREDATOR

At dawn, the cubs asleep, she leaves.
Slowly she walks,
Saffron sun shining on,
Amber eyes . . . gazelles on the horizon.
Her padded feet gently, yet precisely, tap the ground,
The sleepy gait belies her wild intention.
Her tail, a switch that whips the breeze,
Her fur, a golden, rippled rug,
Her scallop ears tremble to the distant calls.

She reaches the sand dune,
Close enough,
Adrenaline rushes in her veins,
Her drumming heart
And pounding muscles,
Implacable gaze fixed on the prey.

The gazelle fawn realises it's behind,
But . . . too late,
The lion cubs will feast tonight!

Matthew Donnelly (11)
The Mary Webb School

BIONIC GRANDAD

My bionic grandad is 72,
He has a pacemaker and an artificial knee.
He has a great sense of humour
And loves to play with me.

He is usually up and about by five,
Making the fire, wellies on and ready to go.
Makes a cup of tea, gets the cows in,
'Nanny, why are you so slow?
Come on Nanny!'

Sometimes he orders me about,
Saying, 'Go up the field, get the Land Rover, get the JCB.'
I don't mind any of these jobs,
As long as Sam, the dog, comes with me.

Oliver Parry (11)
The Mary Webb School

MARCH

As spring germinates,
The snow drops
And the morning sun
Dries the dew.
March flees from
Her hibernation.

Her friendly personality
And shining skin
Bring spirit to her
Bright blue eyes.

The fluffy wisp of white cloud
Is her hat
And the velvety blue sky
Is her soft dainty dress.

She brings life to the meadows
And scent to the air.
When she leaves, there is
No longer a world of ice,
Instead, it's calm
And waiting till next time.

Ky Holder (11)
The Mary Webb School

GRANDAD

Down the drive comes a rumble,
'He's here!' everyone shouts,
Off runs the cat as a car appears,
Out steps a chubby old man
Like a marshmallow, wearing
A cap, trousers and braces.

We go inside, on goes the radio,
Out booms the news
And we know nothing will be the same,
For Grandad's arrived.

Woken at dawn
By the clink of the spanners
And a bang of a bonnet.
Oh no!
Dad's tools have gone again!

Lunchtime comes, the food disappears,
Time to watch the TV.
What is that racket?
Oh . . . it's only Grandad snoring,
Like a pig!

It's time for him to go.
Into the car, off it goes,
Like an old tractor, rumbling up the drive.

There's always something left behind.
I wonder what it is this time?

Jemma Pearson (11)
The Mary Webb School

BIG SIS!

As she strode towards me, the atmosphere changed,
From ice-cold to warm and safe.
Her friendly feelings filled the room
With delight and comfort.
The scent of fragrant flowers lingers around her
Like bees on a honeycomb.

Her eyes are like the hillside on a scorching summer's day,
Shimmering in the light with a deep and dark centre.
Her lips are as red as strawberries and as juicy as cherries
Mixed amongst her cream-like skin.
Her willowy form reaches high for the clouds
With a figure like a snake and her silky hair
Streaked as blonde as the sun.
Fingers like freshly sharpened pencils
Gracefully flutter as she waves at the sight of me -
Her little sis!

Verity Scholes (11)
The Mary Webb School

OCTOBER

As she runs through the forest with her nut-brown skin,
She laughs and the trees move with her and
More come from every direction.
Then she smiles and moves on, pulling the leaves off trees
And drops them on the ground, watching as they stick
To her brown hair and woollen fleece.
She warns people and warns them of the cruel old man Winter,
And she giggles when she sees all the leaves she pulled off the trees
On a bonfire, leaving the trees' fingers bare.

Simon Glover (12)
The Mary Webb School

TYTO ALBA

A heart-shaped face
Belies sharp beak and evil intent.
Cuddly frame veils
The killing machine in side.
In inky blackness,
A strangled screech echoes late into the night.

Ghostly underbody, swooping low, in the headlight's glare.
Pale glow.
Bright white!
Victim does not hear his silent flight,
Unaware of death's presence.
Ears as eyes.
Waits, then slowly flies.

Still,
A strangled screech echoes late into the night.

Connor Grady (11)
The Mary Webb School

MY DAD

As he peers through his glasses,
His pupils get bigger, like a seed beginning to grow.
His beard is trimmed so short,
It's prickly, like a hedgehog.
His moustache is like a blanket,
It covers his top lip to keep it warm.
His chest is like a thick jungle,
My fingers always get lost in it.

His hands are always warm to the touch,
Like the rays of the sun on a hot summer's day.
His hair is soft and speckled with grey,
Just like a small bird's feathers.
His smile is warm and loving,
Like the love I have for him.

Vicki Richardson (11)
The Mary Webb School

PERSONIFICATION POEM ABOUT JUNE

June is filled with colourful flowers,
Her lips are as red as the red roses.
The daisies dance in the cooling summer breeze,
The sunflowers are as gold as the blazing sun.

Her eyes are a brownish-yellow sun,
The sun blazes down like a golden ball.
The sunflowers look like the hot summer sun
And they bring hot air to our village.

She moves swiftly like the summer breeze,
She creates a cooling chill when the wind blows hard.
The trees' fingers touch the ground when the summer wind blows
And then the summer breeze goes and hot air and sun are back.

Her skin is a pale yellowish-gold, with a mix of white.
Her dress is like the silky spiderweb on the dewy grass.
She dresses like an active gypsy,
But slowly she goes and someone beings to make things hotter.

Andrew Keegan (11)
The Mary Webb School

THE BARN OWL

I'm as white as a ghost,
My wings are as long as a road train,
I have a small, heart-shaped head,
I have a dainty razor-sharp beak.

I live in the old rickety barn on the farm,
I'm warm as toast as I snuggle down in my nest of hay,
Day turns into night then I come out for the hunt.

I swoop as gracefully as a dancer,
I fly as fast as the wind,
I dive down on my unsuspecting prey,
Then I fly away and feed on my succulent little mouse.

As the sun rises, I fly back to my toast-warm bed,
In the rickety barn on the farm.

Christopher Ballard (12)
The Mary Webb School

SPACE AT NIGHT

I look out of my window at night, shooting stars pass by.
The world above me is surrounded by all different kinds of monsters,
Scary, sad, spooky kinds.
I've always wondered what the moon was made from,
When I was little, I thought it was made from cheese.
I look up and the moon gives a wink and I wink back.
The planets I like are Mars, Milky Way and the galaxy.
I once thought that you could fly on a twinkling star and travel so far.
The most amazing thing about space, is when Neil Armstrong did a
weird thing.
Space is ace, a wonderful place.

Nikita Soltys (11)
The Phoenix School

SPACE POEM

S   huttling alone around space drifting the Earth, the moon and the sun.

P   lanets in space have beautiful colours and weird names called Pluto, Venus, Mars, Jupiter, Uranus, Mercury, Saturn, Neptune and Earth.

A   ir temperature is freezing, below degrees if you go to space it is really cold but then you come back, re-entry's coming back to Earth.

C   alm Milky Way named after a chocolate bar, in the universe or should I say space, looks so beautiful all the spending and other sparkles like a sparkler.

E   arth is the only planet with humans on it.
In space you can see all the water.
All the green land and all the clouds,
It looks like a giant blueberry.

Shaun Evans (12)
The Phoenix School

ALIENS

Some are slimy,
Some are sticky,
Some have one eye,
Some have none.
Some are green,
Some are blue,
Some have arms,
Some have more than two!
Some are little,
Some are large,
Some have homes,
Some have farms.
This is what I think aliens are like!

Jonathan Hull (12)
The Phoenix School

TILL DEATH DO US PART!

'Till death do us part,' that is what we said,
Some are young boys, but most of us married.
Now they lie there all on the ground, most dead.
I sit alone watching them being carried,
I remember all the happy times,
You're in my head all day long and always,
A man in the trenches always whines.
Others cry and whimper most of the days,
There is blood and guts all over the place.
I can hear the screams of the men in pain.
We all march on, some go at a snail's pace,
Some fall, but get up and march on again.
I hope I am not one of those who will die,
But come home soon to you, my darling Vi.

Holly Deans (14)
The Phoenix School

SPACE ALIENS

S   aucepans flying in the air,
P   lanning slyly in their lair,
A   liens rule the galaxy,
C   reeping high and low round Earth.
E   arth is a new planet, not discovered yet.

A   ngry, but patiently watching,
L   earning to find Earth,
I   t sends a signal about its worth,
E   ver onwards to Earth, to rule another planet,
N   earer and nearer to the planet, but alas, it is Pluto.

Vicki Cork (12)
The Phoenix School

EVERY DAY ONE DIES

Every day one dies, or another,
All I hope is that it will not be me.
Oh how I wish I could see my mother,
But now I know that can never be.
The glory of war has all but gone,
All that is left is the carnage and fear.
None of these boys will return, not one,
Their lives given for a country held dear.
A land fit for heroes was the cry
And as I stand in the mud and rain,
I know that soon is my time to die
And fear my life will be wasted in vain.
The dream that I once held close to my heart
Is as far away now as at the start.

Leanne Gray (13)
The Phoenix School

SPACE

Space is very quiet
With shooting stars
Flying past Mars,
Dark and cold.
Laser-bright sun,
Comets flying through space,
Asteroids all over the place.
Rockets zooming through the galaxy,
The glowing bright moon illuminating the sky,
No gravity, so you can run in the sky.
Green aliens from Mars,
Flying through space.

James Rowley (12)
The Phoenix School

PLANETS' LIFE AND UFOS

P luto is so blue,
L ike Mars is red and the sun is orange.
A re aliens real or make believe?
N eptune and Saturn are part of our galaxy,
E ven the new planet Jeff.
T he sun, Earth and moon are like a triangle.

L ive on Mars and eat some Mars bars,
I n a big volcano crater,
F urther away in the galaxy is the Milky Way,
E at and eat milky chocolate bars.

A nd even the stars are alien technology,
N eptune is bright in the sun's atmosphere.
D arkness rules space.

U nidentified flying saucepans in the sky,
F lying in the morning sky,
O ver the clouds, under the moon,
S ilver capsule in the night sky.

Scott Biddulph (12)
The Phoenix School

PLANETS

P luto is as blue as two oceans put together,
L and is hard on Saturn, it's not nice for a backyard,
A liens eat wheat-like rock on Mercury,
N ippy weather on Neptune, it's getting colder,
E arth's turf is green, it isn't on Mars, it's red,
T iny, slimy, whiny, little blue aliens.
S pace's tastes are horrible.

Jack Welch (12)
The Phoenix School

MY SONNET

There is no glory in the war, it means death.
We are just mere weapons of power and pain.
In the war, I am running out of breath,
This is pointless, I have nothing to gain.
I see bodies covered in blood when I turn,
There are some bodies covered with arms and legs.
Blood everywhere, this makes my stomach churn.
These gas masks don't work, we should just use pegs
There are boys that are too young to fight here.
My best mate was shot straight between his eyes,
Around all of the bodies are some flies.
As the old saying has always gone,
Dulce et decorum est pro patri mori.

Lucy Fletcher (14)
The Phoenix School

POEM OF WAR

War is not a happy place, cold and wet and muddy.
People dying and crying, guns banging,
In the distance, bombs going off,
Blood flying through the air.
Yellow gas spreading everywhere,
Men choking on the strong, yellow gas,
Making them fall to their knees and die in the sloppy mud.
Men coming with lime to put on the dead bodies
To stop the stench of rotting bodies everywhere.
Four years, at last soldiers are reunited with their families.

Tom Higginson (13)
The Phoenix School

THERE IS NO GLORY IN WAR

There is no glory in war, it means death.
We are just mere weapons of war and pain.
In the war, I am running out of breath,
This is pointless, I have nothing to gain.
We have no choice but to fight for our king,
There is no good side to war, it is Hell.
To go home safely would make us sing.
The dead bodies give off a ghastly smell.

I hate to say this, I wish I was dead,
There is nothing worse than to go to war.
I want to go home and lie in my bed,
Fighting for my country is a chore.

Jack Eveson (13)
The Phoenix School

UNTITLED

There is no glory in war, it means death.
We are just mere weapons of war and pain.
In the war I am running out of breath.
This is pointless, I have nothing to gain.
People are dying in the rain.
I am a prisoner in the camp,
I have no friends left in this damp.
The trenches are disgustingly muddy,
I am a time bomb waiting to go off.
The war is really muddy and bloody,
You do not know if you will live through it.
The sound of bombs going off
In my head.

Simon Phillips (13)
The Phoenix School

SPACE

S   pace is a big race, rockets fly
    and stars float up in the sky.
P   lanets nine, come in one big line, it starts at Mars
    because it is not so far, Pluto is last because it is not so fast.
A   liens erupt, they are all green, it wouldn't be hard for them
    to be seen, aliens are green!
C   old and hot planets come, some are big and some small
    and they all come in one big ball.
E   ver, space goes on, never ends.

Louise Pickering (12)
The Phoenix School

WHEN I GO TO SPACE!

When I go to space,
I will be the first face
For the aliens to see!

When I jump from the stars
Aliens will watch from Mars.

Oh, and when I land on Venus,
I will run across its faces.

If I go in a rocket,
I'll put in my pocket
A piece of ground from every planet
I go to . . .

30 years later
My dream never did come true,
I suppose it just got flushed down the loo,
As my job now is a cleaner!

Emma Childs (11)
The Phoenix School

THE SPACEMAN

He walks abroad, again this year
Among the stars,
Tasting meats, tasting beer
Walking fast, walking slow.

His million small eyes
Watching us
From light years away
Wishing he could ride a bus
Or fly an aeroplane.

And now he's coming
Slowly, still staring
His pictures of Earth in his pocket
Thinking that Earth would be full of friends
At peace with everyone else.

Not like war at his home planet
Fighting, killing like a virus on a computer
Killing everyone, nothing but destruction
Earth will be different it decided
A huge light in a universe that's black.

His hundred legs
Keep crashing down
On planets, asteroids and moons
He sees the Earth smile at him
And then disappear just as quickly.

He is a giant in the sky
Wishing that war would die
But as for now he'll just keep walking
Until he feels like giving up searching
Now and forever he'll keep on moving.

If he ever reaches Earth
He thinks this will be the end of his search
The human race will wait for him
The first contact with intelligent life.

But the peace-loving alien will be put in the zoo
And used as a freak in the movies too
He'll never walk among the stars again.

But as for now he'll just keep moving
Until he feels like giving up searching
Now and forever he'll just keep walking.

Mathew Growcott (12)
The Phoenix School

A POEM ABOUT THE WAR

Here I am, standing here,
Bombs dropping,
I have no fear.
All I hear is guns popping,
All I see is people dying,
Lying there on the grass,
I feel like crying.
Soldiers choking on the gas,
The air filled with smoke.
We all run in a hurry,
I try not to choke.
They all start to worry,
'Help me!' I said.
Everyone seems to be dying.

Lianne Wright (13)
The Phoenix School

SPACE

S pace is horrible and creepy,
P lanets are scary and big,
A liens live in space and come down to Earth for a little grace,
C ome to Earth to the birth of a new planet,
E arth is nice, so look after it.

Natasha Balshaw (12)
The Phoenix School

SPACE

S hining stars in the sky,
P lanets covering space,
A gain keeping to the routine, going around the sun,
C ountdown to go to space,
E arth looks small and multicoloured from here.

Janet Boneham (11)
The Phoenix School

SPACE

S tars shine like sunlight,
P lanets look big as we pass them,
A stronauts and aliens fill the sky,
C aught in a black hole we spin round,
E xcitement overrules take-off.

Joshua Corbett (11)
The Phoenix School

SPACE

S   pace is a cool place to visit,
P   luto is one of the planets up there,
A   planet has bright colours that look amazing,
C   ool air, a very spacious place to be,
E   normous stars shine bright and twinkle.

Lanie Davies (12)
The Phoenix School

SPACE

S   aturn sits spinning in space
P   luto pedals far away
A   liens assemble in space
C   rawling, creepy characters
E   very rocket will return soon from the moon!

Abigail Jones (12)
The Phoenix School

SPACE

Space is in the air,
It makes me stand and stare,
Always being such a blare.
I watch the stars as they shine at night.
When I saw a shooting star,
I jumped up with such fright!

Lucy Joy (12)
The Phoenix School

HOME SWEET HOME

There's lots of planets in the world
it would be good to live on them all.
Saturn would be good to live on
to run around the ring.
Mars would be nice and hot
you would never be cold.
Mercury is lovely and bright
you wouldn't need a big night light.
Venus is just as bright
it spins around day and night.
Neptune would be just right
it wouldn't be hot
and it wouldn't be cold.
Jupiter is the biggest one
I wouldn't want to run round that.
Uranus is just so cold
you wouldn't believe.
Pluto is the smallest
just right for one,
but all the planets
have tired me out so I think
I'll go home and get in to bed.

Lucy Phillips (12)
The Phoenix School

SPACE

*S*pace is cool and funky too
My *p*als are coming, will you come too?
*A*ce is space
The planets are big, round and *c*ool
*E*very planet is round and beautiful.

Sarah Smallman (12)
The Phoenix School

GOING TO SPACE

We start in a big rocket,
It goes 3, 2, 1, *blast-off!*
It goes with a big *boom, boom,*
Zooming up in the air, we get into space.
We get out of the rocket,
We start to float in mid-air,
Flying, floating everywhere.
Crunch the moon goes while we walk across.

Running across the planets,
They go crunch, crunch, all the time.
I go across three planets,
I meet four aliens on each of the planets.
'Hello,' I say to all of them.
'Hello,' they say back to me.
'What are you doing?' I ask.
'I am looking for my mummy and daddy.'
'I want to go home,' I say.
I am scared of the aliens.
The rocket has not come yet,
The rocket came up and we went back home to Earth.

Annelise Harris (12)
The Phoenix School

SPACE

S   parkling stars twinkling in the night sky.
P   laces to go, it's time to go in my space shuttle.
A   liens with green skin and hundreds of eyes,
      jabbling on to each other, pointing at me.
C   old, breezy wind brushes through my hair, spacy breeze.
E   arth, back to Earth, tumbling into bed.

Catherine Dixon (12)
The Phoenix School

THE WAR SOLDIERS

Bangs, flashes so close to my head,
All I wish for is to be in my bed.
The bombs, the planes, flying everywhere,
Before I know it I'll be losing my hair.
The Germans are here, they're going to attack,
We're going to find them, there's five in my pack.
I'm face to face with a German recruit,
There's three Germans wearing a clean black suit.
I shot them, I shot them dead,
With blood oozing straight from their head.

Simon King (14)
The Phoenix School

MARS

M ars is the hottest of them all
A ll of the others are like ice cubes to Mars
R eally they say Pluto is the best but I say Mars beats the rest.
S aturn is nothing to Mars the real world.

Michael Thomas (12)
The Phoenix School

SPACE

S aturn sits in space all alone
P luto sits by the sun
A id the alien
C omes to Saturn every week
E ventually Aid goes home.

Craig Hutchinson (12)
The Phoenix School

ON MY WAY TO MARS

On my way to Mars,
I see the stars so high that I think they will touch the sky,
And so high in space I slowed my pace,
I put my face against the window of my rocket to fulfil my grace.

On my way to Mars,
I see lots of coloured circles in a background,
I see lots of rings all different sizes
And then I am looking back at the stars and playing dot-to-dot,
I love this way to Mars a lot and a lot!

Danielle Weeks (11)
The Phoenix School

SPACE

S   tars shining brightly in the sky,
P   lanets, some have no gravity and some do float,
A   liens in space somewhere,
C   ountdown mission control
E   xciting Earth to planets above.

Jordan Anson (11)
The Phoenix School

SPACE

S   tars shining brightly
P   lanets all different sizes
A   stronauts flying through the air
C   omets speeding at 100 mph
E   arth control, we are heading into space.

Sam Hamilton (11)
The Phoenix School

THE GREAT WAR SONNET

It is not a sweet and noble thing to die in a war,
Dulce et decorum est,
It's no good to die for your country anymore,
Pro patria mori,
Being forced into the war was very bad,
Propaganda,
For their families it was very sad,
If they never went to war they would get a white feather

Wilfred Owen was a great poet,
He wrote for anti-war,
Jessy Pope was another great poet,
But she wrote for pro-war,
World War I was very much done,
But World War II was yet to come.

Sean Farmer (13)
The Phoenix School

SPACE

One night I saw a man in a moon,
Eating chocolate bars,
It came as a surprise, he saw a white eye
And said, 'Is that I?'
A rocket came by and said, 'Hi!'
I saw a shooting star,
It looked just like I!
I saw an ugly creature,
I said to myself, is that I?
I saw the sea and said to myself,
That must be the reflection of the sky!

Natalie Dipper (11)
The Phoenix School

THE ALIEN HAS LANDED

The alien has landed with a *bang*.
It came out.
His head was as big as the sun
And looked like a zombie just returned from the dead.
His hand was as scaly as a fish
And his arm was as long as a tree.
His hair was mouldy like out of date cheese.
His legs were as small as a worm
And were covered in blood.
Oh no, he is taking me away
'But why?' I say.

Zachary Brooks (11)
The Phoenix School

SPACE POEM

I like the moon, it's as big
as an air balloon

I like the sun, it shines like
my dad's bum

I like the stars, they make
me stand and stare

I like space, it's as big
as my school place

I like Pluto, it's bigger
than a spaceship

I wonder if I will ever
go up to space.

Stacey Owens (12)
The Phoenix School

THE GREAT WAR

Once lying in the ditch, then getting flung ten foot in the air
Shouts and cries like a baby not getting its toys
Comrade Jones looks like a pile of bones lying in the ditches
We're all aware there are snipers out, they're waiting, waiting for you!
The tanks, oh the tanks so slow and bold, have killed my dad
He was just lying in the ditch, then getting flung through the air
I saw him hit the floor, I dashed to see him, he said, 'Alex, kill me.'
So I got my gun and he lay softly in the mud
This is not a great war; this is not for king and country

It's for the people in the future that will live in peace and honour
I can hear the monsters from under your bed coming to get you and me
This is the last day of the war, only friends wait for me
But today I will not go home. I will go see my dad.
This is the last letter.

Alex Emlyn (13)
The Phoenix School

SPACE!

I wonder, I wonder what is up there so far
From down here it looks like a huge cloud of tar:
   With twinkling stars so bright,
Shining, shining through the night.
   A huge moon as round as a ball
It depends, some nights it might be big or it might be small.
   The whole sky so very black,
Now it's morning but I will wait till it comes back.

Jessica Morgan (11)
The Phoenix School

MY PAIN OF DEATH

There is horror in the night and people crying in pain,
Pain they cry day after day,
People are wounded as the soldiers are slain,
Gassed and drowning in no-man's-land they lay,
The bitter taste of blood, the smell of fear,
As I hang in the putrefying air,
I dream of happy times like drinking beer,
The skies I look upon are bare,
I am not ready to die, I feel scared,
My mind is lost with confusion,
The war is pointless, sadly, I was never prepared,
The last day of the war was just an illusion,
I feel lost, alone in foreign land,
As I tell you this, this is my final stand.

Danielle Leonard (13)
The Phoenix School

STARS

I lie in my bed thinking about space,
how big it is and how mysterious it is.
I climb out of my warm, cosy bed
and tiptoe towards the window,
I slowly open my patterned curtains
and see lots of tiny lanterns
glistening in the pitch black sky.
I smile with joy, but then sigh.
I close my curtains and dive back into my bed
and shuffle right down into the middle of my bed
and wish how I would do anything to go and join them
dancing in the silent sky.

Charlotte Brown (11)
The Phoenix School

SPACE

Shooting
Stars
Dashing
From side
To side leaving
A white trail
Behind them,
Then rockets
100 miles an hour
The sun blinding
You, blazing out.
Plants, Mars,
A chocolate bar
Wishing that you
Could bite into it
Just before lift off
There's countdown
10, 9, 8, 7, 6, 5, 4, 3, 2, 1
The flames going up
To the big black blanket.

Louise Edwards (11)
The Phoenix School

SPACE

Objects flying past,
With a giant booming blast,
Lights are everywhere,
Twinkling like a fair.

Lots of different planets,
All containing granites,
Moon and sun working together,
Making our lives more of a pleasure.

A black hole over there,
Sucking everything out of the air,
An alien traffic jam,
Late for work again . . . *damn!*

Lindsay Donegani (13)
The Phoenix School

SPACE

Beyond the space we will not go
There were aliens a million years ago.

They came to earth in peace and harmony
They laid a human egg in an ape army.

The apes became more suspicious
The eggs hatched and looked delicious.

The humans were becoming more afraid
They looked up at the sky and prayed and prayed.

A thousand years later
Planet Earth had a crater.

Most of the apes were wiped away
The humans were getting intelligent every day.

Humans were getting what they want
Making Earth like a plant.

People come, people go
People wouldn't realise if it were to snow.

So after generations of terrible war
A new era of peace opened a new door.

Daniel Bryson (14)
The Phoenix School

SPACE MAD!

'I've come into space, so far it is colourful, bright and ace!
There are glittery, sparkling stars and fantastic Milky Bars.
I love it up here, I've seen wonderful things
And I might just go and have a look at Mars.
(Seems it is quite near.)
Shooting stars, comets like giant crumbs,
An outstanding sun, oh it's tonnes of fun!'

Jessica Hayward (11)
The Phoenix School

SPACEMAN

S   is for stars, glittering in the dark
P   is for Pluto so far away
A   is for Armstrong, the first man on the moon
C   is for creatures, are they really out there?
E   is for Earth, our true home planet
M   is for moonrock, that silvery dust
A   is for aliens with their weird 20 eyes!
N   is for never, never again.

Lauren Young (11)
The Phoenix School

SPACE IS SO BRIGHT

S   tars and space are so bright,
P   rivate people are still looking at them tonight,
A   ll the astronauts are going into space,
C   ellphones are ringing to say what a place,
E   ast . . . west . . . who knows?

Shaun Smallwood (11)
The Phoenix School

BLAST-OFF !

5, 4, 3, 2, 1, *blast-off!*
Off flies my rocket, gliding through the sky,
Here comes Jupiter, my destination.
Crash! I feel as if I'm being pulled in by the planet's atmosphere,
Suddenly I land, my rocket door opens and I jump out.
Then something flies past me, but nothing shakes,
Everything stands still.
There must be a population living here,
But I don't want to know what it could be.
I get back into my rocket.
Suddenly I float away back to where I won't be an outcast. . . .

Ryan Norbury (11)
The Phoenix School

STARS

S   parkling stars glistening in the night sky,
T   ens of thousands of planets and Earthly creatures surrounding me,
A   liens trying to connect with us human beings,
R   ockets bursting up into the other world,
S   pace is one fantastic thing.

Samantha Jacques (12)
The Phoenix School

SPACE IS COOL

S   is for sun that is a sparkling star,
P   is for planets of which there are many kinds,
A   is for asteroids crashing down to Earth,
C   is for comets whizzing through the air,
E   is for Earth, our home.

Jenna Stones (11)
The Phoenix School

SPACE POEM

Stars shone bright,
in the dark night.
They were so light,
shining in the night.
I got a good view in the sight.
I wanted to see them, my mum said I might.
I looked and looked so hard,
that my eyes were going funny.
My mum called me and said, 'Do you want some money?'
I said no, I was too busy watching the stars,
I thought I could see the planet Mars,
but no, my eyesight is really bad,
but I am so glad.

Ashleigh Glover (11)
The Phoenix School

MY ALIEN POEM

There was an alien with seven eyes
And he was a definite spy.
Which had one nose
Also is a witch I suppose.
He had two arms all scaly and pink
Which is a rainbow I think.
Four legs, all white like sprite,
Teeth all yellow and creamy
And gone all sort of greeny.
Tongue all black and chalky
Don't you tell a porky.
Hair all matted and clattered
Just like this!

Nicole Hickman (11)
The Phoenix School

THE CREATURES

Can you imagine falling off the Earth?
Drowning in a sea of darkness.
Falling past a vast amount of stars,
Falling
   Down!
       Down!
Until *bang!*
Landing on a far-off planet,
Flying and walking around,
They all seem happy
Although they are all different.
Not one of them is the same!
Three eyes, maybe even four,
Amazed as I stared.
Forgetting where I am,
In this distant planet of
Ours.

Katie Murphy (12)
The Phoenix School

ALIEN ATTACK

I met an alien the other day,
The month was in May.
She had a green belly,
That looked like jelly.
She said she was from the moon,
But she looked a bit of a prune.
But then she walked away
And I said, 'Good day.'

Joshua Heywood (11)
The Phoenix School

LIFT-OFF!

5, 4, 3, 2, 1, 0 . . .
The surge of power raced through my body
Ooh!
That was hot,
It was almost burning me.
As I shot through the clouds
And entered the world of twinkling diamonds,
I zoomed, looping around the silver moon,
Suddenly my organs cut out,
I was left floating into a hole of blackness,
I tried to regain control,
But yet,
The force was too strong.
'Houston . . .
Over and out!'

Rachel Smith (11)
The Phoenix School

SPACE POEM

I met a Martian the other day,
Her name was Nesha I'm happy to say.
She was green, she was mean
She was not very keen.
She was big, she was a twig
And had a nose like a pig.
She looked at me and she said,
'I think I have lost my head!'

Tiffany Smart (11)
The Phoenix School

SPACE IS SPACE

Far away on a distant planet,
Is a couple of weirdoes called Ganets.

They own a shop, eyes and spat fingers,
They have six sons, all are mingers.

One has an IQ of an ant,
The other keeps having fights with a plant.

The third, has 17 eyes,
The fourth keeps eating blueberry pies.

The fifth is a pratt
And looks like a bat.

The sixth wears a Parka
And looks like Miss Harper.

So aliens are a couple of laughs,
Shame they are just big naffs!

Alasdair Jarvis (12)
The Phoenix School

I'M AN ALIEN

I'm an alien, I don't know why,
Shooting through space I can fly!
I wonder what that is?
Back there our leader's called Spizz.
On this place called Earth there're UDOs,
And they have things where Homer goes to Moe's!

Nathan Smith (11)
The Phoenix School

THE SPACE POEM

Space is like a black sheet that goes on for miles.
The moon is a football kicked into the sky.
As I look into the sky I see a comet.
I wonder if there're aliens up there getting stuck into the Milky Way?
The stars are bits of glitter blown into the sky.
I've been abducted by aliens into their spaceship.
I thought we were going straight for the sun.
But we didn't, we went zooming into a black hole.
Aarrgghh!

Sophie Davies (12)
The Phoenix School

I WONDER IF?

I wonder if they're blue or black?
I wonder if they smell of fat?
I wonder if they fly around upside down
Or the right way round?

I wonder if they're small or big?
I wonder if they have pigs?
I wonder if they're vegetarian?
I wonder if they go to school?
I wonder if they're mules?

I wonder what it's like up there
Or is it just all bare?
It might just be my imagination
But I swear my grandfather is an *alien!*

Aimee Glover (11)
The Phoenix School

SPACE!

The moon is like a piece of Edam cheese.
The moon is a light bulb illuminating the sky.
The moon is in front of a black velvet sky.
The laser-bright stars all around the moon,
The rockets zoom straight past the moon.
The rockets move softly through space,
Swirling dust floats really calmly past the planets.
Saturn is circling calmly through the night-time,
UFOs go round and round the Earth.
Crusty, crumbling craters crunch.

Hayley Cooper (12)
The Phoenix School

FREDREKO THE ALIEN

He's as scary as a snake,
As big as a bear,
As colourful as a dawn
And as hairy as a hare.

He's got as many legs as a spider,
As many arms as a monster,
As many spots as the skin of a leopard
And a tail like a hamster.

He roars as loud as a lion,
He grunts just like a pig,
He thuds as loud as an elephant
And his hair is as greasy as a wig.

So whatever you do, don't go near
Fredreko the demon alien clown.

Donna Woodvine (13)
The Phoenix School

UP IN SPACE

Up in space,
It's like a black hole,
Pack your suitcase
And climb a pole.

Up in space,
It's very dark,
Cover your face,
Don't bring a shark.

Up in space,
There is a loud rocket,
Get the right pace,
Make your pocket.

Up in space,
You flow in the air,
It's absolutely ace,
Don't mess your hair.

Rebecca Dawson (13)
The Phoenix School

SPACE POEM

Eyes as big as Saturn
    Nose as big as a space shuttle
Teeth as yellow as the moon
    Belly as large as the Earth
Lips as red as his bloodshot eyes
    Hair as grey as Pluto
Bum as blue as Uranus.

Shane Gleave (11)
The Phoenix School

MY SONNET

As I go through the night
    Going through this land
        Trying to see the foundering light
            Keeping myself up to stand.
But as I look back to my men
    But want to say how glad I'm with them
        Only to see standing is ten
            So I say to my men, 'We'll fight until the end.'
Scared of the night, trying to fight
    Hoping to see my mum
        Moving like a horse with his knight
            But trying not to do something dumb.

As I go through this war as people read and adore
    But if they came and saw this is a place of war.

Ricky O'Neale (13)
The Phoenix School

SPACE POEM

The sun is a yellow beach ball
Or a pound coin, a shiny gold marble.

The moon is a silver reflector
Or a ten pence on a black blanket.

The Earth is a blue and green blaze
Covered in fluffy white patches.

The stars are polka dots on a lady's dress
Dancing in the light of a disco moon ball.

Laura Onions (11)
The Phoenix School

MY COLLECTION OF SUPER SPACE POEMS

S   pectacular,
A   mazing,
T   remendous,
U   nbelievable,
R   elish,
N   ormally beautiful

M   anic,
A   mazing,
R   ed,
S   upersonic.

V   enomous,
E   verywhere,
N   ight-time,
U   ncanny,
S   uper-duper.

P   andemonium,
L   unacy,
U   nvelievable,
T   remendous,
O   rion's Belt.

S   upersonic,
O   rion's Belt,
L   unacy,
A   mazing,
R   elish.

S pectactular,
Y ears old,
S uper-duper,
T remendous,
E verywhere,
M anic.

Nathan Pugh (11)
The Phoenix School

DAMIEN THE ALIEN

In space there is an alien
His teeth are big
His name is Damien
He lives in outer space.

In a bit of a weird place
He lives at night
Sleeps at day
Nobody knows if he plays.

His mom is small
His dad is big
He has arms like twigs
His favourite food is salty sligs.

He travels to Earth
To see his aunt Bertha
His two best friends
Me, Bill and Ted.

Time to journey home
To the big, wide dome
His best model is the garden gnome.

Liam Jarvis (12)
The Phoenix School

ALIEN ATTACK

From behind Jupiter,
He rises up,
With a face like a sour apple,
He sets his course for England.

He sent beams down to Earth,
As he set course for England.
We have no saviours,
He gets closer, then you see him clearly.

With beady-black eyes
And octopus tentacles,
With duck-webbed feet
And the head of a dog.

As he touched down,
They all came out
And then the battle commenced,
The men in black were fighting for Earth.

There were beams flying all over the place,
Then all of a sudden,
There was a big explosion.

The alien was no more,
He just exploded in front of agent MK,
Now the clean-up job's started.

Will Sherwood (12)
The Phoenix School

THE MOON

Blast-off to the moon,
We have landed.
Crossing, crumbling, crunching, we walk,
Craters blow up - *boom* - away!

Aliens we meet say hello,
Bang, bang, boo!
The aliens go, in a funny voice.
Off we go, come back soon.

Arron Green (12)
The Phoenix School

EARTH

As round as a ball
Coloured blue and green
It wants to fall
But gravity is mean.

As it spins around
It orbits round the sun
We stay on the ground
While we're having fun.

Day trips to the zoo
Outings to the sea
Rides at Alton Towers
Thank God for gravity.

The moon moves the sea
Then it gets darker
We go in for tea
And we start our starter.

Then we go to bed
All tucked up snugly
So we rest our head
So nice and cuddly.

Stacey Roberts (12)
The Phoenix School

WHEN I WENT UP TO SPACE

Glittery, shiny, silver stars
Against a velvet sky.
Amazing dust that swirls around
Lovely marbled planets.

Golden gems thrown up really high,
Great and so amazing.
Floating round and round in the air,
Crunches beneath my feet.

Steadily moving all around
My feet are swivelling.
The moon is glowing really bright,
Now flashes from the sun.

It is fantastic up in space,
Sparkling and glittering.
Amazing colours everywhere,
Cannot wait to go back!

Sarah Rosser
The Phoenix School

I WONDER, I WONDER

I wonder, I wonder, are there aliens in space?
Because if there are, I think they're ace.
I can see their faces in the stars
I wonder, I wonder, do they live on Mars?
I wonder, I wonder, what it's like on the moon?
Because the aliens might come down too soon.
I wonder, I wonder, what it's like up there?
Do they wear underwear, are they clean?
Are they gooey, are they called Gooey Loowy?

Joseph Ridge (11)
The Phoenix School

APOLLO 2000

Apollo 2000
The fastest rocket ever
It will go past every planet
And around the sun.

It is time for take off
So here we go
5 . . . 4 . . . 3 . . . 2 . . . 1 *lift-off!*
Up and up and up we go
Past the clouds *whoo*
Faster and faster
Higher and higher
Now we are out of orbit
Past Mars, Jupiter and Saturn
We whizz through the ring
Round Uranus
Faster and faster
We zoom past Neptune
Around Pluto
Down past the planets.

Ryan Clarkson (12)
The Phoenix School

LOVE AT FIRST EYE

The space and the galaxy are darker than any
With the raindrops like the stars, we barely see the night
The moon like a milk bottle top, reflecting the sun
I saw her eye glimmering red like a rose petal
Her breath was as coarse as sand
Her lips were like a gravel park
Her leg was crooked like a hill.

Alexander Green (12)
The Phoenix School

THE BATTLE OF THE SOMME

Forwards not back, bent knees; bullets shot past.
Marching through sunshine, humid face of light,
Helmets full of sweat, now see Germans in sight
Officers yelling, 'Lock and load,' don't stop for rest.

Kept with the pace we marched, trembled with fear.
Now reaching German front line, guns firing.
Death struck upon my fellow men, watching them dying.
I picked some earth, could be my last souvenir.

My mind blank, my eyes concealed, deaf as light,
Following the shining candle through the tunnel
Leaving my family behind. 'Mother was right.'
The end was now the beginning, yet shown very dull.

But peace at last, though only a wish goodbye,
A thought in Heaven that mother has not a single cry!

Danny Singh (13)
The Phoenix School

MY GREEN ALIEN

His eyes were as round as the planet Jupiter.
His nose was as pointed as the sharp end of a knife.
Huge ears big enough to fit someone inside of them.
Black prickles for his hedgehog hair.
Three small arms with three fingers.
His large legs, green as grass.
His body is small and round like a football.
Big, jagged, crooked teeth as black as the emptiness of space.
A purple tongue as small as a rubber
But prickly like a holly leaf
And four toes as thin as string.

Conor Edwards (11)
The Phoenix School

A NIGHT IS BORN

The night bird soars across the twilight sky,
Leaving behind its black trail of feathers (it has begun).
The centaur of the sky fires his arrow,
It explodes to become the billions of stars (it is progressing).
The night centaur gallops to release the animal stars,
The baby bear scampers out followed by his mother.
The scorpion snaps and the bull charges,
Into the night sky towards their position (we're near).
The lion is controlled by Orion,
With his faithful dog at his heels (the stars are free).
As they settle for a night all froze in their positions,
Now you know how 'a night is born'.

Rosalyn Halford (11)
The Phoenix School

ALL ABOUT MY ALIEN

My alien is as cheeky as a monkey.
My alien is as colourful as a parrot.
My alien's skin is as rough as sandpaper.
My alien is as brainy as a dictionary.
My alien is as modern as a top clothes designer.
My alien loves music like me!
My alien's smile is like a quarter moon
My alien is as slimy as a big, fat, juicy slug
My alien's slime is like red-hot, slimy snot
My alien's shell is as hard as a house brick
My alien's nose is like a pencil sharpener with two holes in it
My alien's eyebrows are as big as a forest.

Kymberley Beekes (13)
The Phoenix School

ALIEN SIMILE POEM

This creature's lips were as green as the grass.
His teeth were white, just like snow.
His ears were as large as bowling balls.
This creature's eyes were blue like the sky.
His arms were long, as long as a piece of string.
His legs were as straight as sticks.
His tongue was green like a cucumber.

Christopher Hamps (11)
The Phoenix School

ALIEN FROM SPACE

His eyes were as orange as fire.
His lips were as fat as an elephant.
He was as green and as black as a rotten banana.
His hair was as spiky as a hedgehog.
His legs were as skinny as a pencil.
His tongue was as long as the Earth.
His body is a pencil which is as skinny as a pencil lead.

Katie Morgan (11)
The Phoenix School

ALIEN SIMILE POEM

His eyes were as red as a rose and he has six eyes that glow.
His body is fat like a Sumo.
His ears are as big as a rabbit's ears.
He has four arms and hand lasers and webs.
He has six legs and crawls like a spider.
He has a nose like a witch.
His mouth is like a wolf's mouth with sharp teeth.

Daniel Hickman (11)
The Phoenix School

MILKY WAY

Martians in UFOs, eating up the galaxy . . . bar!
In the space rocket, Neil Armstrong goes afar.
'Let's go to the moon!' he said,
'Kim! Watch that stardust! *Use your head!'*
You think space is cool?
Watch Neil and be a fool!
Away he goes . . . crash land.
Yippo the Martian hits him with an elastic band!

Haley Sheppard (12)
The Phoenix School

SPACE MONKEY!

Space monkey
Space monkey
I think he's a space junky
He travels in a space Porsche which is very funky
Getting all the space chicks
Getting out, giving them a kick
When he gets home he is very sick.

Jordon Bolley (11)
The Phoenix School

SPACE

S   is for space like a hole to be filled in
P   is for planet waiting to be explored
A   is for alien looking for a new adventure
C   is for countdown to deep dark space
E   is for excitement as it rattles through your head.

John Simmons (11)
The Phoenix School

ROCKETS

R   ockets go as fast as a wink,
O   utside space is where the planets long,
C   arefully floating through space.
K   aboom, goes the asteroid in space.
E   very astronaut has a white suit,
T   ime is lost in space.
S   omewhere in space there are comets.

I   n space, everything floats,
N   ever to be heard or found.

S   hooting stars whiz through space,
P   luto, the farthest planet,
A   liens want to take over our world,
C   omets crunch through space,
E   T is one of the aliens.

Kimberley Vaughan (12)
The Phoenix School

SPACE

Space is a really cool place
With Martians who live on Mars
Or visit Pluto, the ninth planet from the sun
UFOs are really cool
Who ride through light years.

The planet Mercury is where I stay
Very, very hot here during the day
Neptune looks like a typhoon
So come instead to the moon.

Harry Price (12)
The Phoenix School

CHECKED OUT SPACE

One night I got into bed,
The next minute I was in space.
I checked out the Milky Way
And had a glass of milkshake.
I went to the moon to check it out,
Guess what?
It was made out cheese.
The moon is desolate, lonely, with no breeze.
Then I went to Mars.
Too bad it was not made from Mars bars,
Or is it?
I don't know, I suppose I'll just have to sleep on it.
Now I've gone to my own space called 'dream'.

Donovan Tovey (12)
The Phoenix School

LOST IN SPACE

I'm floating around right here in space,
It's like time has stopped and there's no human race.
Floating in space you can see the planets around,
The rocket I came in has now disappeared,
Now I'm in the darkness that they call space.

The planets are all different colours,
The stars you'll see when you're in space.
The spacemen I see far away,
Walking on the moon they are,
But here I am, lost in space.

Anthony Jackson (12)
The Phoenix School

DEEP SPACE

S   pace is a deep mystery,
P   eople think it looks pretty,
A   steroids pass us by,
C   oldness gets to my nose,
E   arth is my home planet.

M ercury is another 'M',
A   tmosphere is black and blue,
R   ings are like a sandy beach,
S   tars are the light of night.

S   un's heat burns my skin,
U   ranus is not like us,
N   ear the sun is my sunning place.

Shooting stars shine brightly,
Wishing stars cry out,
Comets shoot like people on Venus,
Milky Way pouring milk.

Lesley Hickmans (12)
The Phoenix School

SPACE IS?

Space is a never-ending blackness,
Space is full of flying super stars,
Space is full of flying
And it's full of tar.

Space is when I clear my head,
Space is when I'm lying on my bed,
Space is where I leave my fears,
Is this space between my ears?

Steven Barnes (12)
The Phoenix School

SPACE

I'm lost in space,
Floating softly in space and far beyond.
It's getting hot,
I'm streaking silently past Mars.

The stars are bright, the planets are big,
The solar system is very, very large.
Quickly I'm running to try and get away,
UFOs are after me, quick run!

The moon sleeps like a clown
Floating in black velvet.
I look out and see a star too,
Flying calmly higher and higher.
All the planets slowly moving, quickly they say goodbye.

Stephanie Evans (12)
The Phoenix School

ALIENS

Aliens are green,
Aliens are small,
Aliens go around on the floor.
Aliens are sick,
Aliens are slimy,
Aliens' planet is really tiny.
Aliens can run,
Aliens can fly,
Aliens get shy
When they look at the sky.

Karl Palmer (12)
The Phoenix School

UNTITLED

S   un is hot, it gives us light,
U   nder the sun are nine planets,
N   ever go to the sun, it is very hot.

M   ercury is the hottest planet around,
E   veryone knows it's the first planet,
R   acing in front of everyone,
C   ircling the sun,
U   p above is the hot sun.
R   emember, Mercury is very hot,
Y   es, I was talking about Mercury.

V   enus is where ladies come from,
E   veryone knows this is the second planet,
N   ever forget, you can see me at night,
U   nder the hottest planet,
S   o, never forget I am the second planet.

E   arth is with all the people,
A   ll over the world.
R   ound and round the Earth goes,
T   his is the third planet,
H   eat there is not a lot.

M   ars is good, it's a chocolate bar.
A   liens come from Mars,
R   ight under Earth,
S   o this is the fourth planet.

J   upiter is the fifth planet
U   nder Mars.
P   lanet in the middle of the solar system,
I   t is very big,
T   he biggest planet,
E   ven has the most moons,
R   ather a lot of moons!

S aturn is the sixth planet
A nd uses rings.
T he middle is just glass,
U sing the rings to move
R ound and round the sun,
N ever forget this planet.

U ranus is the seventh planet,
R ound and very cold
A nd no sunlight,
N ever ever higher than 10°C,
U ranus is the third from the end.
S o remember, it is the seventh planet.

N eptune is the eighth planet,
E very day there is no light,
P lanet is very cold,
T here is no sun,
U nder all the planet,
N ever hotter than 0°C,
E very day no hotter than the last.

P luto is very cold,
L ast planet in the system,
U nder the other eight planets,
T he smallest and the coldest.
O ne of the planets you can lose.

Liam Pritchard (13)
The Phoenix School

A DREAM ABOUT SPACE

One night I dreamt about space . . .
I launched off in a fiery rocket,
I landed on Mars,
But it's a shame I haven't got one in my pocket!

Shooting stars, speeding by,
Going through a whirling black hole.
I was extremely scared,
But phew! I have with me my lucky pet mole.

An enormous space rock came rolling by,
Going faster and faster,
Oh no! It's coming towards me, better fly,
To Jupiter! Away we go! I hope I never wake up!

Hannah Elkes (11)
The Phoenix School

SPACE

Floating through space,
Flying on Mars,
Shooting stars,
Moonwalking, slowly,
Circling Saturn carefully,
Running Pluto is so small,
Gripping gravity,
Crunching craters,
Zooming speedily,
Shrieking ships,
Spacy, space!

Wayne Fletcher (12)
The Phoenix School

SPACE

Look out of your window at night
And you will see
The planets floating in a sea of black, night-like water,
With the stars as fish, rippling through the sky
And darting around the planets.

When people say look at the Milky Way
It makes me think that they are getting Milky Bars
From the beautiful sky above.
The sun protecting its children, beams a light,
Slowing burn the Earth!

N o! don't think of planets as huge rock balls,
E veryone knows they are harmless planets,
I t has protected them – the sun,
L oving them and warming them.

So stay away!

Georgina Watton (12)
The Phoenix School

ALIENS

Aliens come in different shapes and sizes,
Aliens come and they speak really weirdly,
Aliens have eyes up high, that's if they have two,
Aliens are slimy and sticky and very small,
Aliens are weird and very creepy,
Aliens have no colour except green,
Aliens are people that are not meant to be,
Aliens are very funny,
Aliens, go back home!

Adam Johnson (12)
The Phoenix School

THE PLANETS

M ercury is like an acorn,
E   verybody knows it is the first planet.
R   ead about Mercury in Books.
C   rumbly, crunching craters crunch,
U   nder Martians' big feet.
R   ound as marbled Earth,
Y   ou should be able to see it from afar.

V   enus is like a piece of popcorn,
E   ver glowing in the sky.
N   aughty aliens try to take over the world,
U   FOs fly by.
S   omewhere in the night you see Venus glow.

E   arth is like a gigantic globe,
A   ll sorts of things live on Earth.
R   ivers are blue, grass is green,
T   hat is what everyone has seen.
H   opefully, Earth is where aliens have not been.

M ars you can see from afar
A   nd it is also named after a chocolate bar.
R   eally weird planet,
S   tars zooming past Mars at night.

J   upiter is like a big ball of fire,
U   nder the black velvet cloth.
P   eople see the planet Jupiter,
I   t is the biggest planet around.
T   ell everyone what you have found.
E   mpire of the aliens,
R   ulers of the galaxy.

S aturn is like a big grape.

A ll round this planet there are rings.

T o me, Saturn is a green apple,

U sing its rings to spin around.

R ound this planet there are moons,

N ice and round like marbles.

U ranus is like a drop of water.

R ound and round this planet goes.

A t night you see it glow.

N ight-time is when it gleams the most,

U nder the sky you see it fly by,

S haped like a yo-yo.

N eptune is like the crunchy snow,

E very day it rotates round.

P luto is next to it,

T ime flies by on this planet.

U se your mask and you can breathe,

N o one can hear you when you scream,

E ven if you wore gloves you'd freeze.

P luto is like a small orange,

L ast in the line of planets.

U nder the sky, Pluto is the last to float by.

T he icy weather on Pluto,

O ccasionally freezes you to death.

M oon is like a 10 pence coin,

O n Earth you can see the moon gleaming.

O n it there are craters,

N eil Armstrong was the first man on the moon.

P   lanets are such amazing things,
L   oads of planets have a wonderful glow.
A   s you fly through the sky,
N   early all the planets you know float by.
E   verywhere you go, you can see planets.
T   ell me more about them.
S   ee Orion's Belt gleaming brightly in the sky.

Amber Rushton (12)
The Phoenix School

I'M ON MY WAY TO SPACE!

I'm on my way to space
A one in a million chance
But it's so cold and dingy
There's no chance of any romance

I can see all nine planets
Saturn, Neptune, Mars
But there's no chance of any chocolate
All you'll get is stars

The stars are bright and glittery
See them sparkling in the night
Oh no there are the aliens
They might give everyone a fright!

My day in space was brilliant
I had lots of fun and joy
And on my way home from space
I bought a little space toy.

Danielle Marie Evans (11)
The Phoenix School

A ROCKET FULL OF POEMS!

Space

Darkness, blinding,
Rockets, finding,
Moon craters,
Star waiters,
Silence,
Nothing,
Black.

Martians

Martians are coming
In their UFOs.
Aliens are coming,
Who are they?
Who knows?

Chocolate space

Chocolate space
Is my favourite place.
Mars is fab
And the Milky Way.
Galaxy's my favourite,
Yum, yum.

The unknown

Space,
A mystery unsolved,
A suitcase full and ready to go,
A mind warp from Mars,
A big, black room with one torch.

Katie Burns (11)
The Phoenix School

SPACE JOURNEY DREAM

Across the empty, lifeless space,
Oh how lonely is this place.
Wait, I see the Milky Way as I curve,
Yuck, they taste much better on Earth.
Gravity makes you feel so free,
Hey, is that Pluto I see?
Little Pluto, away from the sun,
Poor baby planet, you have no fun.
There is Saturn with the wedding ring,
Standing proud like a king.
Look, here's Mars,
I'm not too far
From my heaven of chocolate bars.
Let's go on to Uranus,
The planet that isn't so famous.
Is it green or yellow, I wonder,
Never mind, let's go to infinity and beyond.
Jupiter, Jupiter here I come,
Is it true it takes twelve years to orbit the sun?
You're just slow.
So off I go.
Now there's Mercury with no air,
I know Mercury, it's just not fair.
You sit there and boil,
There's no water and no one loyal
To quench your thirst
Before you burst.

Sorry, we must go whizzing fast,
To Venus, at last,
The planet that shines so bright,
The solar system's night light.

I know how real this may seem,
But wake up, it's just a dream.
Back to a normal day,
Eating Mars bars and maybe a Milky Way.

Lyndsey Pitchford (11)
The Phoenix School

SPACESHIPS

S   omebody help, the aliens are here, they're coming for
P   eople, to eat us all up and to take
A   ll our lovely houses and make them horrible
C   ari, get a gun and blow the five
E   yed aliens back where they came from. 'I've got my tennis
                                    rackets if they will do.'
S   arah are you okay?
H   ey, 'What did you say? I can't hear you. Where are you?'
I   n the rocks and whatever else fell on me, quick hurry up
P   eople are on their way to help. Just stay there.
S   arah, just remember the aliens are still out there. To kill us.

Matthew Haigh (12)
The Phoenix School

THE MOON!

The moon is a boiled potato,
The moon is a silver coin,
The moon is a light bulb in the sky,
The moon is a football kicked up high,
The moon is a face that looks down on you at night,
The moon has holes in it like a mouse has taken chunks out of it,
The moon is so bright, it's like a disco ball shining bright,
The moon is a circle,
The moon can be full, half or quarter, you choose,
Neil Armstrong was the first man on the moon
Or was the first man in the desert, who knows?
The moon can be whatever you want it to be,
The moon is a meteorite that stays in the sky,
The moon is a holy place where lots of creatures go,
The moon is surrounded by lots of stars,
The moon, the moon, I would like to go there one day.

Katie Whitefoot (12)
The Phoenix School

CHOCOLATE UNIVERSE

5, 4, 3, 2, 1, blast-off!
The 'Snickers' rocket zoomed through the Milky Way.
There's a party going on, come on!
It's Chocolate Day!
Everybody's dancing to that funky beat,
Even Mars is out there, now tapping his feet.
The celebrations are out there,
They've been there all day,
All the chocolate stars and planets are there.
Hey! It's Chocolate Space Day!

Chantelle Hicks (11)
The Phoenix School

THE SUN

The sun is a great football on fire,
It is huge and cold,
No, it's hot, I'm a liar.

It's so hot, it would be like you were if
Left in a pan to fry,
Don't get too close, or else you will die.

It is bright orange, yellow and red,
I can see its rays of light through my window
When I am sitting on my bed.

Don't look at the sun with your eyes,
'Cause it will blind you,
As it is dazzling, bright and sphere-shaped in size.

Zoe Evans (12)
The Phoenix School

COLLECTION OF SPACE POEMS

The UFO hid by a swirling cloud,
The ship of a Martian peeking at the planets,
Where do they live? They don't say, they're not very loud.

The aliens zooming,
The rockets looming past the planets in the sky
And lots more up with the planets in that atmosphere.

Mars is a pimple about to explode,
A volcano about to erupt,
A planet in the black atmosphere.

Adam Edwards (11)
The Phoenix School

GALAXY OF SWEETS

I have got a thing for the galaxy of sweets,
You will never forget the galaxy of treats.
The moon is a button, the sun is a ball,
Hanging high and tall.
Don't forget Saturn, the massive shopping mall.

David Emlyn
The Phoenix School

THE MOON IS . . .

The moon is a light bulb in the sky
And is also a football kicked up high.
The moon is a solar powered light
Powered by the sun
And also is a nice and juicy bun.
The moon is very much fun!

Aaron Cooke (12)
The Phoenix School

FLOATING

Floating high in the air,
Going everywhere in my hair,
Flying to a green and blue sphere,
Hey wait I think it's Earth getting near,
I have to go, I got to shoot,
I've lost my lace off my boot,
See you later alligator!

Jessica Brown (11)
The Phoenix School

SPACE IS THE PLACE, ENGLAND

S   pace is a big black cloak that covers over Earth at night.
P   luto is so cold it gives you more than frostbite!
A   ndromeda the star that's hard to be seen.
C   omets crash into planets to be so mean.
E   verything is still when the sun goes down.

Dale Corbett (11)
The Phoenix School

THE BLAZING SUN

The sun is what they call
The hottest star of them all,
Blazing hot most of the day,
But I warn you it is made . . .
Of fire, gas, blazing rock making you
Hot, hot, hot!

Natasha McEntagart (11)
The Phoenix School

SPACE IS . . .

Space is jet-black,
As black as a mole,
A mole as big as a ball,
A ball could be,
The tiniest planet.

Farren Yates (11)
The Phoenix School

PLANETS

Mercury, the bubbling volcano of the planets,
Venus is the brightest of all,
Earth is just a marble ball,
Mars is just a lump of red clay
Thrown on to the black roof,
Asteroids making dents
That are shaped like a hoof,
Jupiter is just a ball of gas,
Saturn has rings made out of glass,
Uranus has got a very long ride,
Neptune is the only planet on its side,
Pluto is so far away,
It takes it years to complete one day.

Edward Frost (12)
The Phoenix School

CRYSTAL CREATURES

Their bodies are as clear as glass,
Their eyes, they are as green as grass.
With sunbeams they create strange lights,
They destroy the comets with unearthly might,
These crystal creatures can surely fight!
With pointy arms and sickle scythes,
These are new horrors of the night,
With crystal teeth and crystal jaws,
With crystal scythes and crystal claws,
These new creatures could be the cause,
Of the first interstellar wars.

Stewart William Harris (12)
The Phoenix School

THE DREAM

I walk along these dark damp rooms,
Stumbling and tripping on every step and mess,
The misty clouds of smoke loom above my head,
The squeaks of mice and rats as I walk a little further
Into the room the noise gets less and less.

Bang, ouch, as I walk into a door,
Boo! Argh! I scream till my throat hurts,
I feel around in my pockets hoping to find a match,
At last I find one and light it.

I light a nearby candle on which I could define as a table,
I look around . . . ah I see a ghost . . .
I sit up. Was that a dream?
The picture stays in my mind of that horrible house,
That horrible dream.

Sara Brazil (13)
The Phoenix School

SPACE

Space, space is everywhere
Down on the floor and up in the air
Rockets zoom through it in the pitch-black
It's like they've been put in one giant sack
Galaxy, Milky Way, yum-yum, very tasty
But be careful of comets, quick get out of there hasty
Visit all the planets way up in the sky
But don't go on Venus or you will die
Neil Armstrong was first on the moon
Or maybe in a desert, you'll find out soon.

Lauren Mace (11)
The Phoenix School

SPACE

S   tars are shining like a strike of lighting,
T   en million I cannot count them all.
A   ny more there will be no
R   oom left in the Universe. Everyone lies down
     looking at the stars.
S   hining in the moonlight in the dark
     when everyone is watching.

Tanya Leanne Whitehouse (13)
The Phoenix School

SPACE!

S   tars shining in the night.
P   lanets glowing also bright.
A   liens looking down from Mars.
C   ountdown happening into the stars.
E   arth is so far *away!*

Kate Ward (11)
The Phoenix School

SPACE

S   tars shining brightly in the sky
P   lants in the air
A   steroids floating in the air
C   ounting down, shaking like mad
E   arth looks small from up here.

Julie Caines (11)
The Phoenix School

SPACE, WHAT IS IT?

Space, it is where most people want to go,
Space, where man is most desired
The world will never forget 1969 -
Neil Armstrong made a mark for mankind.
Space, where they build so many things,
Space does it ever end?

Stuart Rickhuss (12)
The Phoenix School

MERCURY

M ilky Way kid is fast asleep,
E at the whiteness of the clouds,
R ockets exploding crack, crack,
C ountdown stars 5, 4, 3, 2, 1 . . .
U ranus is a planet
R ockets get louder, zoom zoom zoom
Y es, the Milky Way kid is awake.

Kirsty Callear (11)
The Phoenix School

LIFT-OFF

S tars shooting quickly
P acing as they go
A nd as
C urving
E very night watch, they might bite!

Amy Sumnall (12)
The Phoenix School

THUNDERBOLT 3000

Surfing through the universe,
Past Jupiter and Mars.
A spiral round Saturn,
An alien eating chocolate bars.
Pulling the lever giving it some thrust,
Gone through the Milky Way,
I've started to get some rust.
I'm having hallucinations,
Or maybe they are stars,
I'm going home now,
I can see motor mercury cars.

Anthony Richard Peel (13)
The Phoenix School

SPACE

The big cheese,
It's hard to please,
The normal eye,
As you say goodbye,
To the Earth that you knew,
It's half green and blue,
With white whirling, curling mist,
As you grab the lever with your fist
And blast to the moon
And enter the gloom,
The moon is drowned in darkness.

Christopher Horler (12)
The Phoenix School

SHOOTING STAR

S hining like sequins,
H overing over each planet,
O rbitting,
O uter space,
T winkling like precious stones,
I n and out curving past planets,
N ight-time's the best,
G littering like a glitter ball.

S hooting past other stars waving as he goes,
T alking to each one,
A stronauts smiling at him,
R emembered by everyone.

Catherine Price (12)
The Phoenix School

SPRING

Spring is on its way
Bring back a cheerful tune on the way.
Each day goes calmly by,
Silently the sun beams its way,
Gently the night falls.
Slowly the day begins,
Steadily the birds fly,
The trees and grass come back to life,
Softly the birds sing their songs,
Brightly the moon shines.

Babra Yasmin (12)
The Phoenix School

SPACE

5, 4, 3, 2, 1
Into a glistening treasure chest
Thousands of stars perched in their nest
The man a sparkly silver, the sun a fiery red
A shooting star soars overhead
It's all so quiet in this beautiful colourful twist
I go dizzy as I look into the black swirling mist
Pass Jupiter and Mars
Glide past the stars
There is light
Such a wonderful flight
As I soar through the night
The planet behind me is starting to loom
It's time to go back to my nice cosy room
I look through the window and stare at the moon
I've a feeling I'll visit him again, quite soon
Into my rocket I fly through the air
All the weird creatures stop and stare
Pass Pluto and Saturn
They go in a pattern
What a weird place
In outer space.

Kristy Williams (11)
The Phoenix School